Wonder
at the Window

Jaw-dropping moments with God

By Sharon Riddle

The treasures are not the secrets discovered in prayer.
The treasures are the moments spent with Him in prayer.

Acknowledgments

My thanks to...

My husband for trusting and encouraging me many times when I felt I had to do something radical to be obedient to the Lord's voice and for being my best friend!

The Lord for taking me to a wonderful new place in believing Him, although the road made me carsick at times.

Michelle Dudney for editing this book in only three days. Thanks dear friend for using your wonderful gifts.

Marnie for challenging me to finish this book in twenty-one days.

Mary for praying with me week after week. Nothing has made me more fulfilled as a Christian than to seek Him with you. Long after I am gone, I pray you and Beth are walking with the Lord at your window. Thank you too for giving this book cover some style!

Table of Contents

Introduction

He has made His wonders to be remembered. Psalm 111:4a

Blessed be the Lord God of Israel, who alone works wonders. Psalm 72:18

Thou art the God, who workest wonders; Thou hast made known Thy strength among the peoples. Psalm 77:14

Who does great things, unfathomable, and wondrous works without number. Job 9:10

The only times in my life I have been truly speechless have been those times when God did something so amazing, so out of the ordinary, that I could only look on with my mouth hanging open. In this book, the fourth in the series, I have shared some of these awe-inspiring moments with Jesus. As you will see, this book has been about my time in a wilderness of sorts and what the Lord has taught me there. The wilderness is a place far away from ATM machines, fast food providers, and drinking fountains. Yet we find here that God can provide daily manna, water from a rock and whatever we need from out of nowhere.

Perhaps there will be a time up ahead when you will be led through the wilderness. I hope this collection of lessons, scriptures and thoughts will provide encouragement. I am sure there are some jaw-dropping moments ahead for you too.

By awesome deeds Thou dost answer us in righteousness, O God of our salvation. Thou who art the trust of all the ends of the earth and of the farthest sea. Psalm 65:5

Come and see the works of God, who is awesome in His deeds toward the sons of men. Psalm 66:5

On the glorious splendor of Thy majesty, and on Thy wonderful works, I will meditate. And men shall speak of the power of Thine awesome acts, and I will tell of Thy greatness. I will eagerly utter the memory of Thine abundant goodness and shout joyfully of Thy righteousness. Psalm 145:5-7

I remember the days of old; I meditate on all Thy doings; I muse on the work of Thy hands. Psalm 143:5

O Lord, Thou art my God; I will exalt Thee, I will give thanks to Thy name, for Thou hast worked wonders, plans formed long ago with perfect faithfulness. Isaiah 25:1

Chapter 1
Wonder of His Power

How do you explain to someone else the moving, directing hand of God in your life? Some would say that we Christians just do what we want and *call* it the will of God. But that is not true in my life. God has led me to do many things that I would never have normally chosen to do, if guided by my own desires. On some occasions I can recall distinctly hearing the Lord "speak" to my heart. How do you express that to another human being? I did not hear an audible voice, yet the Lord's voice planted a distinct thought in my heart. On those occasions I felt God was saying to do something that was unattainable by my own skill and resources.

One time the Lord told me to start a school at our church. It has since touched hundreds of lives, though when we began there were only eight students. On another occasion, the Lord told me to believe Him for a mission trip to take place that had no human resources. One participant had no passport and had used all his time off from work, neither had shots and there was a specific time frame in which the trip had to take place. Needless to say all these details were cared for, as well as the packing of the containers they would take with them. In each incident, the Lord proved that He was adequate to complete the task He had commissioned. I used to think that the Lord spoke audibly to the heroes in the Bible. He did speak audibly to Moses, I believe, from the burning bush. But I am more convinced that Abraham and others experienced just a pressing thought from God, planted over and over again in the heart. How do you know when the Lord is speaking and leading? How can you be sure you are not just following some personal whim or fancy? The purpose of this book is to serve as a guidebook, a workbook for prayer, which hopefully, will cause you to close its pages and communicate with the One who causes us all to wonder in amazement.

One of the greatest adventures of my life took place when after twenty-nine years of serving in the pastorate; my husband's health forced him to retire. We did not have the full picture of what the Lord was doing in all this. We just knew that Ike was getting weaker and weaker and having more intense pain. We had made as many adjustments to his schedule as possible. Other staff pastors were carrying most of the load. He simply preached. But one Sunday morning he couldn't get up out of bed. We asked the elders of our church to accept this decision, but they wanted at least a three month sabbatical to see if an extended rest would make a difference. Ike spent most of those days in bed. At the end of the three month period he was no better and so, with great regret, we took a path of retirement. One evening as my husband was reading a book about the best places to retire in America, he suggested that we might need to move to another state. He wanted me to read about a few places where house prices and crime rates were low. One of them was Kerrville, Texas. "No way," I exclaimed. "That couldn't be the will of God!" My husband had planted our church and together for over sixteen years we had watched it grow and bloom.

We were attached to our church by a spiritual umbilical cord that we felt went both ways. Surely this could not be God's will for us! My husband pointed out that on a retirement salary, we might need to move somewhere where we could pay for a house out right (possibly out of the profit of selling our current home.) I simply went to prayer and asked the Lord to change the *evil* thinking that had come over my husband. Smile.

A few months later, we began to think that we needed some help in our situation. Ike's condition was not getting better. We could no longer distinguish what the effects were with his fibromyalgia and what were the effects of the medication given to help. We did not have a clue what the Lord was doing with us, and so I began researching on *Focus on the Family's* website for pastoral help. I had done this about a year prior and now for the second time I came across a place for pastors that provided counseling, rest and a place of prayer. It seemed funny that out of all the places in the world, it was located in Kerrville, Texas. We booked a flight for our family of four and looked forward to getting some answers. However, when we finally arrived, the staff was busy with three graduation events and had limited time for us. We found, happily, that the Lord was present and available. My husband and I spent quite a bit of time in the Word and prayer together and separately. I still have the collection of verses the Lord pressed into our hearts during this time of seeking His will for our lives.

There were many things about Texas we liked: the green hills, the calmer, slower pace of life, and the friendly, courteous people. However, we did not think that Kerrville was the place God wanted us to live. As we were driving back to the airport, before leaving, we chose to drive a way we had not traveled before and came through the sweet town of New Braunfels. Located in the Hill Country of Texas, it was beautiful! It felt like the country until you hit the city limits and then, BAM! You found yourself thirty minutes from downtown San Antonio. The housing prices we saw advertised seemed amazing to us, compared to those of California, and so we took the time to check out a few models. The houses were nice. By then I was realizing two things: without a normal family income, we would need to move, and I saw my husband's heart lift a little. He still had pain, but he seemed better able to handle it. It seemed to help him not to have to feel the pressure of caring for others. He was a true shepherd and it hurt not to help others when they needed him. So we began to believe that the Lord might be leading us to move to Texas.

The first thing we needed to do was communicate with the elders of our church the direction we were feeling. Being truly godly men, they wanted the best for us. I believe that they could see the benefit in our move as it prepared the way for the new pastor to effectively minister. The next thing was to tell the congregation. They were shocked, but loved us and wanted Ike to get better, no matter what that required. The third thing we had to do was put our house up for sale. We did this through one of our elders, who was a real estate broker. He and his wife began to walk us through what needed to happen in order for this sale to come about. Twelve years of living in this house had filled it and now, it would need to be cleaned out and downsized in order to look attractive enough to sell. Ike was experiencing much pain and still needed to be in bed, so I began to slowly work my way through the closets, the garage and finally, together we worked through the attic.

I think it's quite humorous how the Lord took us through this time period. We had very little income and so our garage sales accomplished two purposes: they cleaned out our house and they helped us to eat and pay bills. The last thing we sold was my car. It was a difficult thing to part with. For one, it had belonged to my dad. Second, it had been one of the Lord's miracle provisions for our family. Yet, the resource from that car helped us through the last few months in California and was important in the big picture of what the Lord was accomplishing in our lives. During this time we were realizing how unimportant "stuff" was and that things tended to be weights. With the downsizing we were undergoing, we were also experiencing the freedom of simplicity and neatness. It was exhilarating.

In my quiet times the Lord was giving me verses about prosperity, which seemed humorous at the time. I also felt an urgency that we would be moving soon, although we had not had a single offer on our house. I shared this with my prayer partner while we were washing dishes at Vacation Bible School in June. She mentioned that the church was planning a going away party for us in August. I didn't think we were going to be there that long. However, I told her, these were only impressions in the spiritual realm, not anything I could see in the physical. After our conversation, without mentioning it to me, she moved the going away to the last Sunday in July. You will see later how important that move was.
We ended up looking at PODS, which are portable storage containers delivered straight to your driveway. You pack them up and then they are moved to your new location. As I look back on the events that took place, I am overwhelmed at God's work in even the small details of our move.

I had discovered that there was a Christian school in New Braunfels and had inquired about it for our girls. Even though we didn't have any money, I felt that if the Lord sold our house, there might be enough for tuition. He might even want me to teach there to help with our income. Have you ever applied to a school that you have never visited? It seemed funny to begin the process with just so little information, yet I had a peace about the school and a feeling that the Lord wanted our girls there. It went through high school and this meant that they wouldn't need to be changing schools again for a while.

I often checked the airlines for prices during those days, almost daily. But even though my flesh wanted to get us moved, we did not have the money to do it or the peace of God, which is what I have found to be the more important indicator in a "move." However, on July 27th that all changed. I noticed that school orientation was Aug. 17th. I had thought we had until September for all that, so I was truly surprised. I called my husband over to the computer. "If the Lord is asking our girls to change states, churches and schools, wouldn't He at least want them to be there at the start of the year?" We had a time of prayer right then and there and decided to take a step of faith. By then we were convinced that the Lord wanted us in Texas and now we felt we knew that He wanted us to leave. I would order airline tickets and a POD to be delivered the following week. From there on we entered a whirlwind of answers to prayer.

Three days later our church gave us a royal sendoff which made our heads spin. They had been working on gathering a financial gift to care for us in the days to come. We could not believe when they handed us a giant check representing a gift of one hundred and eight thousand dollars. Not a penny of this came from the church, but from generous and sacrificial hearts. After the service, my friend showed me the letter they had mailed out. It said, "The Riddles don't know anything about this and if they did, they wouldn't allow us to do it." That was true.

What a miracle! The eight thousand dollars would be used to move us and set up in our new house. The rest was tucked away in a safe investment that would help provide monthly financial help for the rest of our lives.

Now we surely had the resources to pay for the tickets and the POD, but our house hadn't sold yet. Our real estate agent suggested doing a "staging," which entails bringing   in furniture that most people find attractive. This would mean that we would need to completely clean out our home. The timing couldn't have been better because our POD was arriving on Wednesday. We had a good-bye lunch with the staff that day and a crew of friends from church came after lunch to help load our POD. We finished loading the last few items on Thursday and on Friday the company picked up the POD. Just after they left, the stagers arrived and redecorated for an Open House to be held on Saturday. Our friend and real estate agent, Kim, sat all day on Saturday with warm cookies and pretty balloons, but no one came until just before she left. She showed the house to a young couple and then left feeling a little discouraged.

Later that evening while we were enjoying a good-bye dinner with close friends, we had a call from another real estate agent who wanted to show the house. As incredible as it seems, on Monday morning we had *two* offers on our house. One was a very solid offer from a godly pastor in our city. (I had been praying for a Christian to continue our witness in the neighborhood.) We signed the papers two hours before my husband and girls boarded their plane for Texas. I was left to hand over the car to shippers and board another plane the next morning. The day after I arrived was the day of the terrorist attack in London, so all the airports were shut down. If I had left any later, I wouldn't have made it out for days.

So there we were in Texas, in a Super Eight motel that allowed pets, with four people, a dog and a cat and a whole lot of questions. I began praying immediately for a house to open for us by the time school would start. My husband gently reminded me that although God does miracles, more time is required to actually purchase a house.

Each day we went out looking, inspired by the story of Abraham's servant, who found a wife for Isaac at the well. We reminded God that if He could help a stranger go into a city and run smack into a hard-working God follower, He could help pick out just the right ministry situated home for us. We were also praying fervently that we would be able to find a cheaper place to wait while we house hunted, as the motel was not a thrifty place to live.

We literally visited every housing subdivision in the area, and finally settled on a home in an area known as Mission Hills. But the house would not be ours until September eighth. We had arrived on the eighth and ninth of August. We still had some time yet and the girls were scheduled to start school on the twenty-seventh of August. On one trip out to see our house, we met a Christian lady, Lisa, who had moved from California with her family as well. She told us about some little cottages that were for rent at a much lower price than we were paying for the motel. We took the first available one and moved in the night before school started.

It was indeed a little home. It had a kitchen, so I could cook and we could stop having to eat out. It had a little living room and an upstairs bedroom and bath so our family could again enjoy a little "space." It was thoughtful of the Lord to provide a little home for us by the time school started in His own way. (It's also good to remember that He can answer our heart's desires with His own creative methods of answering.)

This little dwelling was such an answer to prayer. The girls would have had a hard time doing homework in the motel with all the pool activity right outside the door. The Sunday Gruene Haus, as this collection of little "cabins" was called, was peaceful and calm, and brought restoration to our weary hearts and minds. It was there that we met another family from California, the Johnsons, who knew the Lord had brought them to New Braunfels as well. The fellowship with our Christian friends, the Johnsons, in addition to Lisa and her family was so encouraging. We shared several meals and times of prayer together and our kids enjoyed being with each other. These three families have celebrated Thanksgiving together every year since then. We all felt like the Pilgrims that first year in a new land far from friends, church and more; but God cared for us and gave us each other to help provide a sort of mini church for all of us.

Finally, we were able to move into our own home. I wasn't too concerned with moving boxes, but I had prayed quite a bit over two things: moving the piano, which would have to go up several steps, and my harp, which I had prayed would not be damaged after being stored all this time. The weather was HOT and the thought of a fine string instrument being in storage brought a strange temptation to worry. But I had asked the Lord, back in California, if I should sell it and He had replied, "No." On a day when my faith was wavering I asked the owner of a violin shop in town what he thought about it. He said there was no way it would be in good condition. God proved him wrong, I am glad to say.

The day we moved in, our friend Tom arrived to help with the piano, but with Ike not feeling well, we needed more help than that. Lisa, Tom's wife, suggested asking some of the workmen across the street to help. They were willing and the piano was moved. After unloading and examining the harp, I realized it too had come through in perfect condition. There was such a time of rejoicing that evening as we had seen the Lord care for two sizeable requests.

Looking back, we were led along each step by the moving hand of God. We did not walk by the circumstances we could see in the physical, but the ones we saw in our time with Him each day. He did not leave us stranded; He cared for all the details of our lives beautifully.

What did I learn about prayer through all this? First, I learned that I can trust the Word over circumstances. I still have the verses that God gave me during that transition time, and I pray through them regularly I have one set compiled during the three months of our sabbatical.

I have another set that I wrote down when we believed God wanted us to move to Texas, but didn't know for sure. I also have another set that the Lord gave us during the time we looked for our home and asked the Lord for new ministry opportunities in which to pour out our lives.

I want to stop here for a minute and explain how important this lesson of prayer is. When you need to hear the voice of God, the place to hear it is in His Word and His presence. If you are coming regularly to His feet and asking him for wisdom and guidance, He WILL provide the necessary direction. Many times in an ordinary quiet time, he will slip in a clue through a particular verse. It seems to me that the Lord highlights that verse. It just resonates with my spirit and my circumstances. I write these verses out on cards, first, and then later I compile them into pages where I can see more patterns in what He is saying to me. This is the way that I can begin to see themes and where little snatches of text get etched onto my heart for eternity.

These verses become like hand-holds on the mountain climb of faith for me. I don't know what's around the bend, how steep the incline is, or how long I will need to endure. These verses are something for me to hold on to while I wait for the next step in the journey.

Have you ever kept a record of what God is saying to you? Perhaps you have an important decision to make. Perhaps life's circumstances are throwing up everything around you in a "fruit basket upset" fashion and you don't know what your next move should be. Let me encourage you-- God has more than "a word" for you. He has lots of them and you can steady yourself on the peaks of the unknown with them while you wait for His voice to tell you to take the next step up the mountain. A good place to begin is in the book of Psalms. Read until you see a promise pop out and then write it down. As you wait for direction, pray through these verses, claiming their promises and reminding the Lord of what He has said. His Word will begin to soak into your heart and mind, and soon, your feet will begin taking a leap of faith to get you to the next path.

Chapter 2
Wonder of His Plan

My purpose will be established and I will accomplish all my good pleasure, calling a bird of prey from the east, the man of my purpose from a far country. Truly I have spoken, truly I will bring it to pass; I have planned it, surely I will do it. Isaiah 46:10b-11

I began to look for work after our home got settled. But what could I do? That was an interesting question. I had been a pastor's wife for many years. I knew that the gifts that help a pastor's wife be successful would not have much marketable value. I laughed as I considered the skills I could list on an application: I can make a meal for two hundred, pray through the night and lead worship at a moment's notice. Smile.

One area God had used me in the past was as a teacher and I applied at a local Christian school to teach. They didn't have any full time openings left by the time we arrived in Texas, but I got to know the staff and began to get a few calls here and there to sub. I also worked for a temp agency that sent me out on a lot of office jobs where I had a variety of experiences.

It was driving home after a day of working in an office position that I cried out to the Lord, "Lord, this is not what you have called me to do, is it? You called me to be your child, then Your servant, and then one of Your shepherds. Do you really want me to waste my days filing? Please Lord, open up a ministry for me."

Not long after that I got a call that the Christian school had an opening for a teacher in fourth grade. That was exactly where the Lord wanted me for the next eight years. Looking back, he used those preparation days of endless filing for a secular company to build my burden so that I would be assured of my calling to serve Him in ministry and to ask Him for the privilege. When there were hard days of teaching, it helped to remember that this job was my answer to months of prayer. God certainly wanted me here.

While studying the book of Nehemiah, I saw the similarity between Nehemiah's calling and my own. How did the work begin for Nehemiah? Nehemiah had a burden. He was serving in a secular job, but his heart was aching to make a real difference with God's people in God's kingdom.

Now it came about when I heard these words, I sat down and wept and mourned for days; and I was fasting and praying before the God of heaven. Nehemiah 1:4

Nehemiah asked God to open up the way and this was the same prayer that I prayed as well. In my case, the fourth grade teacher was going to have a baby and didn't feel she could keep up with the physical demands of teaching. I smile to think that months before this job opened up God HAD heard my prayer and His answer was already on the way. I just had to trust Him and be patient as I waited for the answer that had been *conceived* to grow in time. That's an important thing to remember when you are praying over anything.   God does hear and He moves. It's just that we are not always able to see His response until later when it becomes apparent in the physical realm.

But certainly God has heard; He has given heed to the voice of my prayer. Psalm 66:19

And I said to the king, "If it please the king, and if your servant has found favor before you, send me to Judah, to the city of my fathers' tombs, that I may rebuild it." Nehemiah 2:5

When we make ourselves available to God, He takes us seriously. When we are ready to get down to business with Him and surrender all our personal preferences and silly quirky demands, He responds with opportunity. He always has a place for a servant. This is something He has shown me over and over again. If we need a name plate over the door, lunch delivered and awards handed out, the opportunities may be few. But if we are willing to scrub floors in His name or reach out to hurting people, our doorbell won't stop ringing.

There have been times when what the Lord wanted me to do was something that I didn't feel particularly gifted to do. It might have been out of my comfort zone or my faith zone. This is why, on some occasions, the Lord has used a steady day to day message to act like a soaker hose in getting His Word into my heart and to build up my faith muscle. At the same time, He has built a burden for that particular ministry to which He is calling me.

Perhaps this is where you are right now. You want to be

used by God, but you are handing Him a timetable of when it would be convenient for you to be available. Or perhaps you are listing the kinds of jobs you're willing to do or feel comfortable doing. You might not be ready for God to use fully, yet. He may wait until the burden grows and you finally cry out, "Use me. Lord. I'll do anything, go anywhere, suffer anything, as long as you'll put me in Your service and accomplish something for Your glory."

The task God had for Nehemiah had been monumental. It was going to be one of the most demanding things Nehemiah had ever believed God to accomplish. It was so important to God that he had chosen a fully devoted servant to face the challenge. It would require, not only all that Nehemiah could believe God to do, but it would also require the dedication of everything he possessed to see it to the finish line. Have you ever been prepped for such a task?

Looking back there are some similarities to working at a Christian school. Christian school employees are probably smiling right now as they read this. The physical demands of teaching can be rigorous, but the commitment to financial sacrifice can be just as real. God knew that He needed to get all of me on the altar. I had to be a desperate woman. I needed to be desperate enough to do anything that would accomplish His will. He knew how to build a burden. For me, it was endless days of filing, realizing that my gifts and callings, as well as a seminary education, were being wasted. For Nehemiah, it was serving cup after cup, and thinking about the city of God lying in ruins, dreams heaped over by rubble, and the people of God in chaos.

"...And a letter to Asaph the keeper of the king's forest, that he may give me timber to make beams for the gates of the fortress which is by the temple, for the wall of the city, and for the house to which I will go." And the king granted them to me because the good hand of my God was on me. Nehemiah 2:8

When God is in the process of building a burden or a vision, you can be assured that He is guaranteeing the resources to finish the task. Whether it is building a wall, leading a nation through the wilderness, feeding five thousand, or starting a brand new ministry, if God is calling you to something He wants done, He will provide what you need to complete it. And because He has declared it, it will be done. There may be a period of laboring over the required resources in prayer. For Nehemiah it took four months. But if God has called you to do this, then the guarantee has already been issued for all the resources that will be needed.

And Abraham called the name of that place, The Lord Will Provide, as it is said to this day, "In the mount of the Lord it will be provided." Genesis 22:14

Whatever the Lord pleases, He does, in heaven and in earth, in the seas and in all deeps. Psalm 135:6

But our God is in the Heavens; He does whatever He pleases. Psalm 115:3

For He spoke and it was done. He commanded and it stood fast. Psalm 33:9

Your God has commanded your strength. Show yourself strong, O God, who hast acted on our behalf. Psalm

Commit your way to the Lord, trust also in Him, and He will do it. Psalm 37:5

Commit your works to the Lord, and your plans will be established. Proverbs 16:3

Nehemiah recognized that God had put this idea in his head. He began to survey the city and assess the damage. And the Lord began to plant a vision for fully restored walls and relationships. Step by step directions began to build in his brain. So too, the Lord would plant thoughts in me for lessons, chapels and more.

Often, I realized, these insights came at the end of my prayer time. I began to notice the spiritual activity that occurred directly after my time in His Word and His presence.

And I arose in the night, I and a few men with me. I did not tell anyone what my God was putting into my mind to do for Jerusalem and there were no animals with me except the animal on which I was riding. Nehemiah 2:12

Then my God put it into my heart to assemble the nobles, the officials, and the people to be enrolled by genealogies. Nehemiah 7:5a

Who puts ideas into your head? Some thoughts are put there by God. Others, in an attempt to snare us, are planted by Satan, and finally, there are some human thoughts that we just think randomly ourselves, or come from others.

Satan's ideas are pretty easy to spot. They promote self-indulgence, laziness, greed, and comfort. They turn us away from times of worship, fellowship, prayer and the study of God's Word. It is more difficult to discern the difference between God talking to us and our own random thoughts. I think that looking at my prayer journal helps me realize the difference between the general nature of my ideas and God's: Nehemiah aptly describes human ideas as inventions of the mind.

Then I sent a message to him saying, "Such things as you are saying have not been done, but you are inventing them in your own mind." Nehemiah 6:8

Here in essence, is the difference between my ideas and God's ideas. My ideas are always changing and quite scattered. They are usually very attainable and sometimes, they are abandoned as quickly as I think them. God's ideas are like a seed that grows until it bears fruit. They can be outlandish, but many times are just quiet, practical ideas. And here is one more quality of God's ideas: they always get completed. Sometimes they even get done in a flash; so quickly, they make your head spin. Other times they take centuries, so those that see their fulfillment have to look back to the writings of others to see when they were first uttered.

A few days ago I was thanking the Lord for an avenue of spiritual encouragement for me. Dr. Tony Evans has many messages on a Christian app called, Right Now Media, that I have been enjoying each day. On this particular morning, the Lord prompted me to thank Dr. Evans for the way his messages have strengthened me, and as I was searching for a means to communicate with him, I saw that he was speaking THAT night, at a dinner for pastors in Houston, hosted by radio station, 100.7 FM, The Word. The information said that the dinner was sold out, but there was a little button to click if you wanted to be added to the wait list. My heart cried out to God for a chance to hear this particular message and I clicked the button and filled out my information. Not long after that I received an email from Brian, at the radio station, telling me that not only were they booked, but they were over booked. They had four hundred and ten people signed up to fill three hundred and fifty spaces. I thought to myself, "If God wants me there, He'll make a way, and if He doesn't want me there, I don't want to be there anyway."

It wasn't ten minutes later that my phone rang and I could see, by caller ID, that it was coming from Houston. I said, "Brian, do you have two tickets for me?" He said that as a result of the weather, he had received a flurry of cancellations and that yes, we could come. Imagine when I walked in and let Ike know all that had just gone on…God had given me my heart's desire. We hurried to prepare to make the journey (a six hour round trip.)

When we got to the Houstonian Hotel, where the event was being held, we had the wonderful opportunity to meet and talk with Dr. Evan's personal assistant and to let him know how much Dr. Evans had encouraged me during this time. We sat at a table with pastors who were planting churches, and the Lord really used my experienced church-planting husband to encourage them. We enjoyed a beautiful meal for free; one that cost one hundred and fifty dollars per person, and the Lord empowered my husband to physically make the demanding journey. Usually the daily pain he endures limits his driving to about two hours at a time.

Ideas that come from God are totally un-doable by human standards, but accomplished easily with His power and for His glory. I don't mean to imply that God's work is always easy, only that His work, done His way, in His time, gets done. (This thought was first spoken by Hudson Taylor, a missionary to China in the eighteen hundreds.)

His purposes grow within us steadily, and sometimes, with a little push from God's pinky, the landscape changes overnight. There are no limitations, financial, physical, spiritual, mental or emotional to the work He wants to do, and so a lot of things can change instantaneously when it is His will to do so.

It is like a mustard seed, which a man took and threw into his own garden; and it grew and became a tree; and the birds of the air nested in its branches. Luke 13:19

And the Lord said, "If you had faith like a mustard seed, you would say to this mulberry tree, 'Be uprooted and be planted in the sea'; and it would obey you." Luke 17:6

Seeing a lone fig tree by the road, He went up to it and found nothing on it except leaves. And He said to it, "May no fruit ever come from you again!" At once the fig tree withered. Matthew 21:19

Ah Lord God! Behold, Thou hast made the heavens and the earth by Thy great power and by Thine outstretched arm! Nothing is too difficult for Thee. Jeremiah 32:17

For nothing will be impossible with God. Luke 1:37

And He said to them, "Because of the littleness of your faith; for truly I say to you, if you have faith as a mustard seed, you shall say to this mountain, 'Move from here to there,' and it shall move; and nothing shall be impossible to you." Matthew. 17:20

Once the work has begun, then the enemy tries to stop it. His intention we are told in Nehemiah 6:2 is "to harm." He uses four key methods.

Then Sanballat and Geshem sent a message to me, saying, "Come, let us meet together at Chephirim in the plain of Ono." But they were planning to harm me. Nehemiah 6:2

One way Satan tries to stop the work of God's people is through disheartening the workers. He simply reminds us of information that is somewhat true.

And he spoke in the presence of his brothers and the wealthy men of Samaria and said, "What are these feeble Jews doing? Are they going to restore it for themselves? Can they offer sacrifices? Can they finish in a day? Can they revive the stones from the dusty rubble even the burned ones?" Nehemiah 4:2

All who see me sneer at me; they separate with the lip, they wag the head saying, commit yourself to the Lord; let Him deliver him; let Him rescue him, because He delights in him. Psalm 23:7

The enemy whispers things in our ear like, "You can't make a difference. You can't build a wall. You're not strong enough." These statements have an element of truth to them. Without the Lord's help, it would be impossible to accomplish many of the tasks the Lord assigns His servants.

Thus, in Judah it was said, "The strength of the burden bearers is failing, yet there is much rubbish; and we ourselves are unable to rebuild the wall." Nehemiah 4:10

For all of them were trying to frighten us, thinking, "They will become discouraged with the work and it will not be done." But now, O God, strengthen my hands. Nehemiah 6:9

Another one of the best tools the enemy uses to stop the work is conflict. I've seen him use it on me and on others. In Nehemiah's case, he used HOW the Israelites treated each other to stall the work of rebuilding the spiritual fiber of a nation. The wall had already been completed by this time. Some Israelites were buying others to use as slaves. Some were charging high interest on loans to their fellow countrymen. Nehemiah could see that this was no way for brothers and sisters to act.

Again I said, "The thing which you are doing is not good; should you not walk in the fear of our God because of the reproach of the nations, our enemies? Nehemiah 5:9

How many times in the body of Christ do we see that conflict has disrupted the work of building the Kingdom? There are certainly times when an issue, either personal or corporate, needs to be addressed. Sometimes sensitive matters must be confronted. But the spirit of love must blanket every action, and prayer must be under every step to protect the hearts and minds of His people. We are all human and will all mess up from time to time in what we say, but if we are listening to the Holy Spirit and getting things right with each other, the Lord will be glorified, even in the way we handle "mess ups."

A side note on this topic is that, yesterday, I was able to participate in a conversation that brought resolution and peace to a situation of conflict after twenty years. Praise the Lord! My advice is…don't wait twenty years to have these kinds of conversations. I could have deactivated the enemy's torture if I had only handled this sooner. Think of all the wasted worry and hurt that could have been avoided!

Another method the enemy uses is distraction. I cannot tell you how many times the enemy has tried this on a Wednesday afternoon with me. I have taught Bible study now at my current church for eight years and always attend the meal offered by our church prior to the lesson. Often in the afternoon, the enemy will point out something, an errand, or a fun thing that I've been meaning to do. "You can do that and still get to Bible study." But early on I made a commitment to the meal time and the fellowship that occurs there, as well. I know that the enemy sees the power of loving on people before you try to teach them anything. So Satan will always try to throw a curve ball into that process. I had to treat this aspect of fellowship like a paid job I do for God. "No, this day is consecrated to the Lord. There will be enough time for all that on another day," I say. And there always is plenty of time later on. The urgency is just spiritual warfare from one who likes to distract.

So I sent messengers to them, saying, "I am doing a great work and I cannot come down. Why should the work stop while I leave it and come down to you?" And they sent messages to me four times in this manner, and I answered them in the same way. Nehemiah 6:3-4

They enemy also tried to get Nehemiah to leave the work, not permanently, just for a few hours or days or months. If he had gone, that delay would have had deadly consequences to the vital job God had entrusted him to complete. My friend, God has entrusted you with a great work. It may seem to be very simple, like having a consistent family devotion time, or setting a certain time aside each day or night to pray. But this particular job God has given you to do cannot be done by anyone else. It is strategic in God's plan and He is counting on you to complete it. Distractions are deadly. While you are getting off track, the enemy is moving in on things in the Heavenly realm. We must recognize the detours he offers and turn away from them; we must go back to our calling.

The last main tool I want to mention is that the enemy likes to use fear. He tries to use a paralyzing fear that can grip us, and although it can have many different faces, its root can always be traced back to fear.

If you are a people pleaser, he may use the thought that you might let someone down to stop you in your tracks. This is a good tool for the enemy to employ on godly and gifted people, who are making a difference in the kingdom. If you love people, sooner or later he will bring this tool out of his arsenal.

If you are driven by accomplishment, he may use a fear of failure to set you back. What if you try your hardest and the wall is still not completed? What if you sacrifice all your personal resources and it's still not enough? He will whisper in your ear to end the work quietly before you see public humiliation.

If you enjoy the honor of a good reputation, he may try to mess with that somehow. Someone may spread untrue rumors about you or allege that you have done this or that. A helpful tool during this time will be to mentally put your reputation on the altar as a sacrifice to God. Give it to Him, along with your life as a gift. It will totally disarm the enemy and his plan.

He can take fear and dress it up in all kinds of scenarios to get God's people to give up. We must recognize his craftiness and respond as Nehemiah did when he saw fear in himself and others. We must look to the Captain of the Host to fight this battle and to worship Him while we wait to see the victory.

He was hired for this reason; that I might become frightened and act accordingly and sin, so that they might have an evil report in order that they could reproach me. Nehemiah 6:13

When I saw their fear, I rose and spoke to the nobles, the officials, and the rest of the people: "Do not be afraid of them; remember the Lord who is great and awesome, and fight for your brothers, your sons, your daughters, your wives, and your houses." Nehemiah 4:14

Nehemiah reminded himself and others of two important messages in his book. The hand of God is on you (see Nehemiah 2:8b), and the Lord is great and awesome (Nehemiah 4:14, 9:31, 32).

Whenever fear tries to take over, we must focus on the

Lord and remember that His hand is on us and on the work which He has called us to do. We must also remember who He is and what He is like. He is great and awesome. One of the key ways we do that is to praise the Lord, even before we see the victory.

In the summer of 2013, just prior to Vacation Bible School at our church, we found out that our youngest daughter's college bill for the year was going to be eighteen thousand dollars. Our resources were pretty much tapped out by sending our oldest to college for the two years prior to that. The timing of this information was almost humorous. That year I was leading the Bible Drama Center at our church's Vacation Bible School and preparing to teach the Word to almost one thousand children. It was a big job and required all my attention. I remember sharing this with my team that week and asked them to praise the Lord with me like the Israelite choir singing before the battle despite this overwhelming need. We did.

Worship is a deadly weapon against fear because it turns our thoughts on to the only One who can help. I remember consciously making a decision when fear would come over me to turn and worship the Lord, individually and corporately.

Later, after Vacation Bible School had gone beautifully, we found out that every penny of her bill had either been covered by scholarship or loans. Praise the Lord!

Do you see why the enemy wanted me to be fearful? A great work would have been diminished. So too, he will try this on you. Get a playlist of worship songs ready... powerful praise songs to meet his attack and focus on the power of God. Be ready. This attack will come.

Then Ezra blessed the Lord the great God. And all the people answered, "Amen, Amen!" while lifting up their hands; then they bowed low and worshiped the Lord with their faces to the ground. Nehemiah 8:6

And it came about when all our enemies heard of it, and all the nations surrounding us saw it, they lost their confidence; for they recognized that this work had been accomplished with the help of our God. Nehemiah 6:16

In addition to praise, Nehemiah had some additional offensive action to counteract the enemy's weapons of disheartening, conflict, distraction and fear. One is that he stationed everyone in a family. These were spiritual units of encouragement. Nehemiah knew that everyone would need the strength that comes from encouraging words: "I'm praying for you." "I'm here for you, brother." "We're behind you all the way, sister." This concern only occurs when we are in a small group environment, sharing our weaknesses and struggles. No one is strong all the time, but as we get close with others, there will be times we are the encourager and times when we will be the one encouraged. It's a wonderful plan the Lord designed to strengthen us for battle.

Then I stationed men in the lowest parts of the space behind the wall, the exposed places, and I stationed the people in families with their swords, spears, and bows. Nehemiah 4:13

As for the builders, each wore his sword girded at his side as he built, while the trumpeter stood near me. Nehemiah 4:18

Nehemiah also reminds the people that they must always be aware and have their weapon ready. One of our greatest weapons is prayer, but we need to remember there will be lots of moments that will require us to unsheathe and use it. We might be standing in the grocery store and hear a friend tell of a recent trial. Take out your weapon. Hold that need up before the Father.

Picture a magnificent Marine, dressed in full uniform and armed to the hilt. Suddenly, there is an attack, but he stands and tries to talk his way out of the danger at hand. Forget it! Get out the bazooka! Let loose the hand grenades! Use your weapon, friend. That's why it has been issued to you!

Nehemiah also wants us to see that there are going to be times when the trumpet will blow to alert us to come together and stand as one man. Individually we can be defeated, but when we all stand, arm in arm, linked together in perfect harmony, we create a full barrier against the attack of the enemy. We are always our strongest when we are hearing and responding to God's Word as the body of Christ.

And all the people gathered as one man at the square which was in front of the Water Gate, and they asked Ezra the scribe to bring the book of the law of Moses which the Lord had given to Israel. Nehemiah 8:1

Then on the second day the heads of fathers' house-holds of all the people, the priests, and the Levites were gathered to Ezra the scribe that they might gain insight into the words of the law. Nehemiah 8:13

So in disheartenment, in conflict, in distraction and in fear, take out your weapons. Get stationed in a family of believers who will fight with you. Get some praise on, take out your weapon of prayer and use it. Let's stand together as a corporate body and listen to God's Word and then obey it. No matter what you have been assigned to complete, God will hear and answer you with a mighty victory.

Now at the dedication of the wall of Jerusalem they sought out the Levites from all their places, to bring them to Jerusalem so that they might celebrate the dedication with gladness, with hymns of thanksgiving and with songs to the accompaniment of cymbals, harps, and lyres. Nehemiah 12:27

And on that day they offered great sacrifices and rejoiced because God had given them great joy, even the women and children rejoiced, so that the joy of Jerusalem was heard from afar. Nehemiah 12:43

Be glad in the Lord and rejoice, you righteous ones and shout for joy, all you who are upright in heart. Psalm 32:11

Chapter 3
Wonder of His Promises

The Lord has been mindful of us; He will bless us. He will bless the house of Israel. He will bless the house of Aaron. He will bless those who fear the Lord the small together with the great. May the Lord give you increase, you and your children. May you be blessed of the Lord, maker of Heaven and earth. Psalm 115:12-15

I want you to think of yourselves as Abraham and Sarah. We can each remember the moment when God first called us and told us to leave the land of self and pride and come to the promised land of relationship with Him. We remember the step of faith we took in our hearts to meet Him at the altar of forgiveness and begin to walk His way. We remember the moment when we thought for the first time, I believe. God remembers it too. He knew the moment we believed even if it was only a moment of personal reflection that no one else heard or saw. He set us on our way to a new life, a new way of thinking, a new hope. Like Hebrews ll:15 says, if we had wanted to return, there were plenty of chances along the way, but the promised life was worth everything we had to leave behind.

Much of what God promised Abraham was not even for him to hold in his hand, but for him to believe for the generations to come. He was a spiritual mid-wife of sorts for future generations. He saw it "from a distance" and believed, yet they were the ones who actually got to claim the real estate of what had been promised. That's the purpose for this chapter. I believe that the Lord wants us to stake a claim through faith for the generations who are yet to follow us. I believe that there are some concrete things we can do that will affect those who will come next in line.

First, we must understand why we can expect God to do the same things he promised Abraham. Romans 4:16 tells us that we are his descendants by faith:

*For this reason it is by faith, that it might be in accordance with grace, in order that the promise **may be certain to all the descendants**, not only to those who are of the Law, but also **to those who are of the faith of Abraham**, who is the father of us all,*

We used to sing the song, "Father Abraham." I wondered what significance the title had. It just seemed to be a silly little song. But now I realize that I am his heir and can expect an inheritance of those things he was promised, just as Isaac and Jacob did.

What are some of the things Abraham believed God to accomplish? First, Abraham believed his descendants would exist. It seems rather odd to me that Abraham was asked to believe promises for descendants even before he had any of them. Day after day and year after year he faced the barrenness of his own inabilities and yet he believed God.

He was one hundred years old and his wife was past

menopause before he ever saw that promise become reality. In other words, he had to walk in the confidence of grandchildren before he ever saw a son. Some of you can already easily picture your future through grandchildren and great children. But others of you are straining to see how your faith will affect children and grandchildren you don't even have, or can't have at this point.

Sometimes God likes to remove all the human possibilities before He displays His awesome God-power. I think it is interesting that Sarah, Rebekah and Rachel were all barren, yet they all birthed children of promise. Here is the key: God already knows your children, your grandchildren, your great grandchildren...and their great grandchildren (should the Lord tarry). Now this might be easy for some of you to believe. My friends Mike and Robin, parents of six, might have an easier time picturing "descendants" than someone who faced the possibility of none...like my friends Chris and Lou. They received the answer of a son after many years of praying. Also, my friends Marc and Rachel could not have children until the Lord opened Rachel's womb and gave her three strapping young sons. We used to pray regularly around an abortion clinic and often asked the Lord to give her children. He answered, "Yes!" Can you believe now for those who will follow you?

That the generation to come might know, even the children yet to be born, that they may arise and tell them to their children, that they should put their confidence in God, and not forget the works of God, but keep His commandments, Psalm 78:6-7

This will be written for the generation to come; that a people yet to be created may praise the Lord. Psalm

Abraham was also asked by God to believe that his descendants would multiply. He was asked to believe that his seed would multiply more than the sands of the sea or the stars in the sky. Can you believe for the many as you look at the few? Can you believe for the hundreds and thousands who will follow as a result of your spiritual parenting even if right now it doesn't look like anybody wants to follow your spiritual course?

I recently re-told the story of William Carey's life to a group of students. William was a poor cobbler with little prospect of even feeding his family, let alone changing the world. He answered God's call and spent five years in India before he saw a single convert, yet when he died he had started one hundred and twenty schools. George Mueller, who lived by faith, saw the Lord begin over one hundred schools through his ministry and cared for thousands of orphans. But at the beginning of his ministry, he had to believe for just one orphan.

Can you begin to get the "Big Picture" of what the Lord might want to do through your life and in your city? Let's encourage our faith by taking a moment to count the stars. They are the heavenly abacus God wants us to use when we think about His children and the future. Do you get it yet? Can you see the enormity of what the Lord has planned for your family and ministry?

"And I will establish My covenant between Me and you, and I will multiply you exceedingly." Genesis 17:2

And He took him outside and said, "Now look toward the heavens, and count the stars, if you are able to count them." And He said to him, "So, shall your descendants be. Then he believed in the Lord...Genesis 15:5-6a

Abraham was asked to believe for the Promised Land. He was promised all the territory of Canaan, and yet Acts 7:5 tells us:

And He gave him no inheritance in it, not even a foot of ground; and yet, even when he had no child, He promised that He would give it to him as a possession and to his offspring after him. Yet his descendants received all of it because he believed.

The Promised Land was a promise made to Abraham on behalf of those yet to be born. Yet it was HIS FAITH that brought it about. Can you believe God for the territory, and yes, even the physical land that will be needed to teach those who will come long after you are gone? Can you look at a barren land full of corruption and idol worshippers and claim soil for God worshippers who will one day travel these roads? Can you believe for the land that will be necessary for the multitudes we have just pictured? The Lord spoke to Joshua hundreds of years after Abraham and said in *Joshua 1:3:*

Every place on which the sole of your foot treads, I have given it to you, just as I spoke to Moses.
It's not faith to expect God to provide enough land for what we see right now. We need to be able to believe Him for land for what we cannot see yet at all. If our faith gets fenced in to this little piece of property that we call our abilities...woe be unto us. God wants us to think outside the fence. He wants us to see the world as His backyard. He said: *"Ask of me...and I will give you the nations."*

God also asked Abraham to believe Him to protect those that were His own. God cared for and protected Lot because of Abraham's sake. He sent an angelic team to escort Lot and his family out of Sodom, and Genesis 19:29 tells us that He did it specifically for Abraham's sake. For the children of promise there are no limitations on what God will do.

Thus it came about, when God destroyed the cities of the Valley that God remembered Abraham, and sent Lot out of the midst of the overthrow, when He overthrew the cities in which Lot lived.

Oh to cultivate such a love relationship with God that He remembers us and cares for those we love with such attention. We don't know what our children will face. But we can say with certainty, that whatever it is, God will show compassion on them, for our sakes, and protect them from the plans of the evil one. II Peter 1:9 tells us:

Then the Lord knows how to rescue the godly from temptation, and to keep the unrighteous under punishment for the Day of Judgment.

Abraham believed that God heard his prayers for all that were his. God blessed Ishmael specifically because of Abraham's prayer of blessing.

And as for Ishmael, I have heard you; behold, I will bless him, and will make him fruitful, and will multiply him exceedingly. He shall become the father of twelve princes, and I will make him a great nation. Genesis 17:20

We don't know a lot about Ishmael. We know he was a rebellious man *"who settled in the Havilah ... in defiance of all his relatives." Genesis 25:18*

We don't know anything that would make us think he had a relationship with God and yet, he is blessed of the Lord. Why? Simply put, because Abraham asked God to bless him. The important point not to miss here is that when the godly pray over their descendants, God is listening and active. When I used to bring my kids to school, I always sent them off with these words, "Be a blessing." Every morning as I pray for my own children I ask three things for them…that they be useful, fruitful and faithful to the Lord.

All day long he is gracious and lends; and his descendants are a blessing. Psalm 37:26

"They shall not labor in vain, or bear children for calamity; for they are the offspring of those blessed by the Lord, and their descendants with them. Isaiah 65:23

Abraham believed God to provide a future godly spouse for Isaac. When it was time to find a wife for Isaac, Abraham was not physically able to "go select one." Yet we see confidence as he commissions his servant to blindly set out on the road to a distant land. Why? He had asked the Lord to provide the right one. When the servant entered the city, Rebekah was the first young woman he encountered. God had selected the needle in the haystack. Rebekah had character. She was hard working. (She brought the sheep every day to water them at the well and she offered to provide drink for all the servant's camels.)

I also believe she had to be a woman of great faith to leave her family and marry a man she had never met. We read later that when her twins struggled within her, she sought the Lord to find out why. The Lord knew He was preparing a lineage of faith. He saw her faith muscle and hand selected her out of the crowd to be the wife of the son of promise.

Can you believe for godly spouses for your children and their children's children? This will be critical to future generations walking with God. Without godly spouses it will be doubtful to have godly children. It is totally in line with God's will, but we must still ask Him for it. Do you believe He can and will do it?

He believed God to introduce Himself to future generations and to bring about their spiritual awakening. It seems believable that Abraham could affect Isaac with his spiritual influence. He had day to day contact with him. But how could he affect the generations that he wouldn't have the chance to rub elbows with? Do the math. He was one hundred years old when Isaac was born. Isaac was forty when he married, but his wife was barren for a while. She was barren until he prayed for his wife to conceive, which shows us how important our prayers are in bringing about the things God has promised us.

Jacob and Esau were born when he was sixty. Abraham died at one hundred and seventy five. He probably did know of them and possibly met Jacob and Esau and might have even known them until age fifteen, but how could he affect Joseph and Benjamin, Judah and the rest? How could he touch and influence them to worship the Lord?

Abraham was promised his descendants would bless the world. *In you all the nations of the world will be blessed.* Of course God knew that from Abraham's line would come the Messiah, but also, He knew that the world as a whole would be blessed through God's people. How could God promise that? Doesn't each man have free will? How could God know for sure that the descendants of Abraham would follow God's way? Here is the critical point I want you to see. God is taking on the responsibility of introducing Himself to the descendants of Abraham before they are even born.

*"And I will establish My covenant between Me and you and your descendants after you throughout their generations for an everlasting covenant, **to be God to you and to your descendants after you**. And I will give to you and to your descendants after you, the land of your sojournings, all the land of Canaan, for an everlasting possession; and **I will be their God.**" Genesis 17:7-8*

"The children of Thy servants will continue, and their descendants will be established before Thee." Psalm 102:28

We see this lived out in the life of Jacob. As a young man he is a deceiver, but God introduces Himself to Jacob at Bethel. Interesting, isn't it, that this is one of the first places where Abraham ever built an altar and called on the name of the Lord! Abe's altar of prayer became Jacob's ladder to Heaven. Do you realize that every day we come to our altar of prayer, we are building Heavenly meeting places where future generations will be introduced to God?

And the Lord appeared to Abram and said, "To your

descendants I will give this land." So he built an altar there to the Lord who had appeared to him. Then he proceeded from there to the mountain on the east of Bethel, and pitched his tent, with Bethel on the west and Ai on the east; and there he built an altar to the Lord and called upon the name of the Lord. Genesis 12:7-8

My altar of prayer can be effective hundreds of years from now. And God can take our sons and daughters and turn them into fully devoted followers of Christ. It might be easier to believe for a million dollars, rather than to believe what I just said about your son or daughter given the current condition of their lives. It's easier sometimes for me to believe that God can build a building than to believe he can rebuild a rebellious life. He can do both!

Remember Judah, Abe's great-grandson who didn't keep his promise to his daughter in law, Tamar? What about Simeon and Levi who killed an entire city because someone raped their sister, Dinah. To ALL of Abraham's descendants, God makes this marvelous promise:

"If his sons forsake My law, and do not walk in My judgments, If they violate My statutes, and do not keep My commandments, Then I will visit their transgression with the rod, And their iniquity with stripes." But I will not break off My loving kindness from him, nor deal falsely in My faithfulness. My covenant I will not violate, nor will I alter the utterance of My lips. Once I have sworn by My holiness; I will not lie to David. His descendants shall endure forever and his throne as the sun before Me. It shall be established forever like the moon, and the witness in the sky is faithful." Selah. Psalm 89:30-37

God doesn't want me to believe He can save my children based on their ability to be good, but on His ability to be God. God is in the business of turning deceivers and murderers into patriarchs. Do you believe He can do this for your children? Can He do it for your grandchildren? What about for their grandchildren? Perhaps some faces of current family members just came to mind. Perhaps they are not God worshippers right now. I have great encouragement for you from another fact from Abraham's life.

Abraham had to trust the Lord to return his family from the enemy's hand. There is a small incident in Genesis chapter fourteen where Abraham comes home to find that he's been robbed. All his people, including his nephew Lot have been taken captive, as well as many of his possessions. We read in Genesis 14:14 that:

When Abram heard that his relatives had been taken captive, he led out his trained men, born in his house, three hundred and eighteen, and went in pursuit.

Three hundred doesn't seem like that big of a force when fighting an army, but Abraham didn't see it that way. He probably would have taken off after Lot with three men as long as He felt confident that the Lord was on his side. We can't "out faith" the Lord, no matter how big our faith is! Now listen to the promise of Isaiah 42:18-22:

Hear, you deaf? And look, you blind, that you may see. Who is blind but My servant, or so deaf as My messenger whom I send? Who is so blind as he that is at peace with Me, or so blind as the servant of the Lord? You have seen many things, but you do not observe them. Your ears are open, but none hears. The Lord was pleased for His righteousness' sake to make the law great and glorious. But this is a people plundered and despoiled; all of them are trapped in caves or are hidden away in prisons. They have become a prey with non to deliver them; and a spoil, with none to say, "Give them back."

He wants you to wake up to the possibilities of all the descendants you've already given up on that are held in the enemy's grasp. The Lord wants them back in His fold. Are you willing to mount up and pursue from this moment forward? Do you believe?

Build an altar and call on the name of the Lord. Start praying now for the salvation of the son or the brother who is a captive. We must pray. It is the only tangible construction tool we can use that can reach beyond our physical span of life. It is the only device that can hit a target we can't even see. It is the only combination to open a heart locked up tightly.

His mercy is upon generation after generation toward those who fear Him. Luke 1:50

Can you believe God to reveal Himself to future generations because of *your* faith? Abraham believed God to prepare places where future generations would meet Him. We can build altars through our prayers that can help lead the next generation to find Him and follow him. Jacob built an altar at Bethel. Joshua set up stones in the Jordan. These were spiritual markers that said to the world, *God met me here.*

A spiritual place can be as simple as a cow pasture. I recently received an invitation to attend a former church's one hundred and twenty-fifth anniversary. This was a church my dad pastored from the time I was in fourth grade until I was a freshman in high school. As I thought about all the pivotal things that happened in my spiritual development during those years, I realized how much I needed to show my gratitude to the people of that church.

During those years I became a believer, and I consecrated my life to full time Christian service. I developed my love for music and worship. During this time I got my first sewing machine and began to make my first projects. I also developed a love for the Word and for prayer during those years. Many of those spiritual road markers took place at a camp we would attend every year that was held in an old cow pasture in Santa Cruz, CA.

We didn't have a big fancy campground but God blessed us anyway. One of my close friends became a pastor and another became a professor of theology at a Christian university. You see, God can take *any* physical place and turn it into a greenhouse for His purposes. Our walk with God makes the place fertile and able to make it grow lives that honor Him.

Later, as I began to teach, I would pray for the same spiritual progress to take place in my students' hearts. I realized that much of what they would do for God would get started in my fourth grade classroom. I wanted my prayers to water their hearts and the Word to condition them to hear the Holy Spirit's voice. And like Abraham, I believed MY faith could even affect their choices.

Over twenty five years ago, I worked preparing a video, with others in my denomination, on Light and Life Christian schools. As I researched their long list of schools in Southern California and investigated how they began, I saw a theme. The people who began the Light and Life schools in Escondido, Azusa, L.A., Chino, Barstow, Sylmar and Fontana all had something in common—no one had much money. These schools were started in houses or Sunday School rooms. In preparing the history of these Southern California Schools, the thought that repeatedly struck me was that no one had the resources to begin such a task. In fact, by our standards today they might have even been considered poor. No one had extra time. No one had the high education required to begin such a venture. Yet today these schools stand as spiritual markers of what God can do when men and women trust Him. Why? These men and women believed God for what was needed to do the work. Can you believe with me tonight, that the Lord will begin some greenhouses around where you live for growing world- changing Christians?

When I first entered the classroom several years ago, I saw a lot of needs. We began praying and God began answering. We needed a TV, a VCR, a laser printer for the computer lab, a portable hard drive, puppets, a drum to use for worship, Christian story tapes to use during handwriting practice time. Anything we needed and asked Him for, God provided. You know how it is for *you* and *your* children. If there is something they need, you get it for them. Picture the Lord. He is loading up the shopping cart at the back to school sale night. He wants this generation to be prepared for what lies ahead. He will spare no expense in creating the faithful character they will need to stand strong.

Here is the kicker, however. We may be able to believe

for tangible items we think future generations might need like buildings and land, but how about inner character that might be needed to meet persecution? How about tenacity? How about boldness? How about endurance? Start praying now. The scripture passage the Lord gave me to believe in the year 2014 is this:

*By faith, Moses, when he had grown up refused to be called the son of Pharaoh's daughter, **choosing rather to endure ill-treatment with the people of God, than to enjoy the passing pleasures of sin, considering the reproach of Christ greater riches than the treasures of Egypt;** for he was looking to the reward. By faith, he left Egypt, not fearing the wrath of the king; for he endured as seeing Him who is unseen. Hebrews 11:24-27*

This passage shows me some incredible character that had been grown into Moses. He chose ill treatment over pleasure. He considered reproach for Christ's sake more valuable than the treasures of Egypt. He didn't fear the wrath of the King, but he feared God as if He was standing right there. Wow! Can you see the ramifications of praying this over your future generations? Wouldn't this generation need that kind of faith, considering what we have already seen happening in the news?

God wants us to believe that He can prepare those who follow for what they will face. Our family recently watched *The Hiding Place* again, which is the story of the life of Corrie Ten Boom. She and her sister were prisoners of war during WWII who were arrested for helping Jews escape. Here was an example of God's richest treasures being mined under the most brutal of circumstances. We don't know if our children will face this kind of persecution, but we must believe in the God who can do anything—even preparing and sustaining them through intense difficulty.

Don't you get it? God can do anything! He used a barren woman to begin the line of promise. He used a virgin to conceive His Son. He stopped one star in motion, the sun, to win a battle and birthed a new one to guide the wise men. He overcame death in a grave. There is nothing too difficult for Him!

He can take a rock and turn it into a sanctuary. If He says a school, or a church, or a life will be built, it will be built. He could use a blind man to build it, a deaf man to lead its worship, a mute man to preach His message and a lame man to start the dancing. Or, he could use you and me crippled by our inability and insecurity to do it.

It's not your money, your skill or your time that will accomplish God's purposes—oh how limited those resources would be. What He is very interested in is your faith. Do you believe that He can do it? Do you believe He will do it? The essential building block is faith. Are you laughing, rather smirking, like Sarah, or do you believe? God can see right down to your faith muscle. You can't fool Him.

It's not your intellect that will determine what He does. You don't have to know *how* He can part the sea or make water come from a rock. You simply have to take your stance of belief; then watch and pray.

In 2003, I stood and asked the students of our school in California to believe God to give them something they could give to the school. In my heart, I asked the Lord to give our family ten thousand dollars for the Olive Branch Community Church and School. Within a year of that prayer, the Lord gave our family four times that amount to give in an incredible answer to prayer.

You don't have to be able to see *how* God can grow and expand His school in the midst of a stalled economy. You must simply believe that He knows how to do it. You don't have to comprehend *how* He is going to care for your family in the generations to come. You just have to believe that He will. Look at what God did through one man who believed. Think what He could do with all of us in a state of active faith. Do you believe? Keep in mind that there are also consequences for disbelief:

Then they spoke against God; They said, "Can God prepare a table in the wilderness?" Behold, He struck the rock, so that waters gushed out, and streams were overflowing; can He give bread also? Will He provide meat for His people?" Therefore the Lord heard and was full of wrath, and a fire was kindled against Jacob, and anger also mounted against Israel... Psalm 78:19-21

In spite of all this they still sinned, and did not believe in His wonderful works. Psalm 78:32

They did not remember His power, the day when He redeemed them from the adversary, Psalm 78:42

...who gives life to the dead, and calls into being that which does not exist. Romans 4:17b

If you belong to Christ, then you are Abraham's offspring, heirs according to promise. Galatians 3:29

...for He who promised is faithful. Hebrews 10:23b

*O God, Thou has taught me from my youth; and I still declare Thy wondrous deeds. And even when I am old and gray O God, do not forsake me until I declare Thy strength to **this** generation, Thy power to all who are to come. Psalms 71:17-18*

For the eyes of the Lord are upon the righteous, and His ears attend to their prayer. I Peter 3:12a

Chapter 4
Wonder of His Preparation

God can prepare us for a situation completely unknown to us. A few months ago, I was meditating on Hebrews chapter 11 and began to focus in on the words of verse seven.

By faith Noah, **being warned by God about things not yet seen,** *in reverence prepared an ark for the salvation of his household by which he condemned the world and became an heir of the righteousness which is according to faith. Hebrews 11:7*

There is a lot going on in this verse. First, we have Noah, with an active faith, ready to hear the Lord's voice and to follow through on what he hears. Then we have a faithful God preparing Noah for something up ahead that Noah has never encountered before. It's a wonderful combination, one that will always produce spiritual fruit, but not without some faith-producing tension.

God somehow communicated directly with Noah to let him know the specific dimensions for the ark, the materials it would be made of and the directions that would make it a seaworthy vessel. This is remarkable to me. Noah was not a builder that we know of. The text gives us no clues to believe that Noah had any experience with a hammer. This is as incredible to me as if I walked into the garage, lifted the hood of my car and starting making repairs. Oh my!

There is a clue in Genesis chapter six of how this extraordinary task was accomplished. It is the same way you and I will be able to complete the work given to us through God's Spirit: Noah walked with God. He maintained daily intimacy with His Heavenly Father, who possessed all the data necessary to help him successfully cruise through the peril of a world-wide flood.

But Noah found favor in the eyes of the Lord…Noah was a righteous man, blameless in his time; Noah walked with God. Genesis 6:8, 9b

We know that Noah was a human being, so he was not sinless. We know that he had sinned because we have all sinned and fall short of the glory of God. We can assume, as well, that he made mistakes because of his humanity. I can picture one day where the gopher wood piece was cut too short or the pitch compound got left with the lid off and Noah had to re-do the day's work. There had to have been days where he lost his temper, perhaps with his family stuck in cramped quarters for almost a year on board the ark, perhaps during the days, weeks, and months that he preached to the unrepentant bystanders. But here is the key. In the midst of sin and humanness, Noah is counted as blameless. How can this be? The answer is in the last part of the verse: *Noah walked with God.*

I can imagine that Noah began and ended his day talking to the Lord. I can imagine an ongoing relationship with God where God could examine Noah's heart and bring to mind corrections to be made, confessions to be voiced and more. I know how the Lord does this for me. He sifts through the day's events pointing out a harsh word or an impatient spirit.

The task the Lord was going to give Noah was going to require mental ability as well as spiritual desire. Noah was going to have to be equipped to head a building project ahead of his time, captain a ship at sea and become a zoo keeper for a collection of species bigger than any in existence. Yet God was able to prepare Noah to accomplish all of it.

You are Noah, my friend, and I am too. Around the corner are events that we have never faced before, challenges we have never dreamed about, and yet, we can confidently face them because we walk with God. He is the one who is able to prepare us for them. He can prepare us spiritually. He can strengthen us physically. He can even stretch us mentally to complete a task.

I recently experienced this for myself. After teaching at a particular school for several years, the Lord through a series of events spoke and told me to resign my position. This is not an ordinary thing to do in Sept. of a new school year. However, by faith, I obeyed. Looking back in my prayer journal is so astonishing, it's hard to believe. On Oct. 1st I had a meeting with my principal to discuss the situation. On October 3rd he accepted my resignation. Sandwiched in between those two occurrences on Oct. 2nd was a Skype call with a company in the Netherlands for whom I now write interactive white board lessons. Go figure! God was preparing me for a time of working at home and writing this book, as well. It is amazing to me that He laid out the steps so carefully.

I want to make sure that you don't get the wrong impression, however. Working part time for the last several months at home has not been easy. Because I am hired by the job, my paycheck does not come on a regular basis. I have no guarantee of future work and my first check required me to wait over two months. During that time, however, the Lord has done something unique in my life. He has encouraged my faith muscle, He has given me a contentment that has cut down on my shopping impulses, and He has shown me countless ministry opportunities that have been opened to me as a result of working from home. This, plus the fact that He has drawn me close to His presence has made these past several months a wonderful faith adventure. But it hasn't been "easy."

Trust in the Lord with all your heart and do not lean on your own understanding. In all your ways acknowledge Him, and He will make your paths straight. Proverbs 3:5-6

God communicated practical matters with Noah like how to prepare food for the family and the animals. (6:21) He instructed them how to pre-plan for the care and survival of every animal. (Genesis 6:19-20) He even told how many of each animal to take. Noah did according to all that the Lord had told him to do.

God even communicated with Noah exactly when they were to enter the ark. There were seven days of faithful waiting before the rain began. These days of waiting were very important as a picture of faith for us. I wonder what they did for seven days with no rain, but lots of animals. When did God shut the door? When they first entered the Ark, or seven days later on the day He caused the rain to come. Maybe he gave them seven days in which to worship and perform spiritual warfare through prayer and fasting. I know from experience that God loves it when we are following a faith trail and we just rest in Him and rejoice even though there is no answer on the horizon. Many times when God tells us something, there is a little period of waiting between the telling and the fulfillment. It's the window where our faith is tried and we learn to stand on His Word. One of my favorite verses during a period of time like this is Psalm 131:2-3

Surely I have composed and quieted my soul; like a weaned child rests against his mother; my soul is like a weaned child within me. O Israel, hope in the Lord from this time forth and forever.

As our family waited on my first paycheck, this verse became especially meaningful to me. The company kept promising that my pay would arrive in a few days…in a couple of weeks and so on. We had been waiting almost two months and my hubby was beginning to think the job might be a hoax. Some particular moments of faith came first, at our church's Thanksgiving service where we praised the Lord publicly, and then on Thanksgiving Day, when our family gave thanks to Him privately. My pay arrived the following day. I was grateful for the resource, but even more, that I had heard God correctly and was following the path He had for our lives.

That's one thing to remember about hearing the voice of God: You believe you've heard Him, but there can always be a twinge of doubt until what he is saying is confirmed. The hardest thing is to obey when there is no immediate feedback that you heard correctly.

I can just imagine Noah and his family sitting in the ark with all the animals waiting day after day. Ham, or Shem might have gotten restless and started playing tag football. Noah's wife may have thought of a couple more items for the to-do list. Noah just had to get alone and pray, "Lord, if I heard you correctly, then please send the rain. If I'm wrong, then please somehow use this situation for good and Your glory." If Noah had disobeyed what he believed God was saying, his family would have died. The consequences were real.

If the future of your family and perhaps the world depended on your obedience, how would you do? Your obedience to the revealed will of God is critical. Do you wonder what the difference is between people God uses greatly and those that just seem to tread water spiritually through life? It is this one point. The ones God uses greatly are the ones that follow through on what they believe God is saying.

God depended on Ananias to go over to Straight Street and pray for Saul. Obedience on another occasion would not have worked. Elijah needed to press for rain through prayer on one appointed day. Obedience at another time would not have completed God's purpose for a national revival. What if Joseph had delayed forgiving his brothers to another occasion? What if Jesus had postponed submission to His Father's will in the garden? The consequences of your and my obeying the voice of God is no less essential.

But Noah obeyed all that God told him to do. God directed all the details, even down to where He wanted the ark to land. He brought Noah and his family safely through the most cataclysmic event that had ever taken place in the world and brought them out to thank and praise Him.

When Noah and his family stepped off the boat, they were in a new world, but one with less fear. After all, they must have thought: "He got us this far, how can we not trust Him for what's up ahead?" I'm not sure what you are going through, or about to go through, but I know this: God can prepare you to face it and get through it to the other side where you can thank Him under a rainbow of fulfilled promises.

Chapter 5
Wonder of His People

This past year I received a copy of my family heritage compiled by a distant cousin. There was a powerful story about my Great Great Grandpa. His name was John Pitto Johnson (meaning son of John). He changed it in later generations to Newland, my maiden name, when he immigrated to the United States in the 1880s. When he grew up he was WILD. He got the nickname "*Wild* Peter" in the community in Northern Michigan. The family history did not list the *wild* things he had done to earn this handle. It just said that this was how people related to him and the kind of man they knew him to be.

One day he struck up a conversation with a man at the grinding mill who invited him to come to church and eat a meal with his family the next Sunday. *Wild* Peter was not at all interested in going to church, but as he was new to *Amerika*, he was interested in getting into an American home, so he accepted the invitation. In the course of the service, the Spirit of God moved on the congregation and John gave his heart to the Lord. His life completely turned around, so much so, that he began to be known as *Godly* John.

I was so impressed by hearing about the man at the mill who invited him to church. His name was Carmi Parker.

The story goes that he was an individual who struggled with being tongue tied. God actually used a stutterer to declare an invitation that set our family's course in a whole new direction. Then, the Lord used a small Free Methodist church, which was a simple log structure, to be the place of His anointed transformation.

There was nothing noteworthy about this little church except that its people stayed enough out of the way long enough for God to work that morning. It's what they didn't do that is significant. They didn't quench God's Spirit. They didn't offend the visitors or make it hard for them to come and hear the message of forgiveness. And then, they gave this *wild* man a chance to change his ways and his reputation. All these things are important parts of "church growth" that we sometimes miss.

It is interesting that after his conversion, he then influenced a line of other kinsmen who passionately loved God: His son, Andrew became an ordained elder and pastor. His grandson, Albert, my grandpa, and four other grandsons became ministers. My father and two other cousins became pastors as well. Of his great, great grandchildren, two became missionaries and four more became ordained ministers.

So the story is more interesting because one man inviting another man to church changed the course of six generations and continues to do so. This story particularly highlights those who became ministers in my family, but many more were just godly laymen and women who led by example in their churches and families, were devoted to prayer, and loved God deeply.

Let's stop here for a moment and ponder what happens when God's people obey? The world changes, sometimes overnight.

There have been some people God has used to change my world overnight and others He has used to change my world over the years. One of the first was a children's evangelist named Julia Mae Weber. She was a single lady with a passion to reach children for the Lord. I loved her puppets, Ocrat and Ecan. She usually had a contest in every church where children had to guess that their complete names were *Republican* and *Democrat.*

We learned memory verses to earn little white cards which could be cashed in for plaster of Paris creations and other prizes. In those days, fun events for children were few and far between, and her coming to our church was akin to the circus coming to town.

When I later became a children's director, I pondered from time to time, how did she practically do this from one church to the next? I'm sure it was *by faith.* How did she afford all the wonderful prizes she gave for memory work? She probably did what most called to children's work do; she most likely paid for them out of her own resources.

Much later I inherited her plaster of Paris molds. She had given them to my mother, Mary Newland, and I felt I had a sacred trust to carry on. Those molds were used many times with the children I had been entrusted to teach. Her ministry impacted my life greatly and even now, like Elisha, I pray for a double portion of her "spirit" in my teaching.

Another person that greatly impacted my life was a

youth minister, another single lady devoted to the Lord, Linda Bakke. I remember that even as a busy teacher with many responsibilities to fulfill, she would meet the youth of our church BEFORE school to pray regularly. I also remember her taking me along on a shopping trip to Gemco. Though the trip might be insignificant to some, it proved that she cared about me and allowed her to deeply impact me during a significant growth time in my Christian life. Never underestimate the significance that can take place when you show God's love to a child. If I can remember being taken on a shopping trip, think of how God can use you doing some simple act of love for a youngster, as well.

There are others who impacted me, some who will never even know it. At the camp where we attended each summer were several people who taught ukulele, music conducting and sewing classes. They poured time into some scrawny kids like me. It is amazing how something simple like that made such a difference in the course of my life and the lives of my close friends. Many of them ended up in ministry because of the loving examples of Christian living that went before us. Two of us went on to become music majors and those conducting lessons really helped when we all got into Al Clift's conducting class at Azusa Pacific University. Thanks, Reva Hart, for giving up your vacation time to teach us ukulele. That helped when we hit Music Theory class and needed to understand chord progressions. A couple of us are now life time quilters, but we got our start in Mrs. Thorsen's sewing class on those hot afternoons in a simple cow pasture.

What kind of legacy are you leaving behind? You may be tongue tied, but you can invite someone to church and a meal. You may not play at Carnegie Hall, but you could teach a little class at church or camp that might change the lives of five or six youngsters. Your call might be to rise early and pray before work, but whatever it is, know that your example, prayer and faith may change the next several generations to come.

Chapter 6
Wonder of His Process

There is an interesting thing that happens when we consistently honor the Lord with our lives. He promises that over time, the spiritual landscape changes. Sometimes the change is even reflected in the physical and emotional landscape as well. I am not arguing that sometimes it can take years to see the transformation, but sometimes it happens in minutes like when Mt. St. Helens erupted during my time in seminary in Oregon. Meditate on this passage from Psalm 107:33-43:

He changes rivers into a wilderness and springs of water into a thirsty ground; a fruitful land into a salt waste, because of the wickedness of those who dwell in it. He changes a wilderness into a pool of water and a dry land into springs of water; and there He makes the hungry to dwell, so that they may establish an inhabited city, and sow fields and plant vineyards, and gather a fruitful harvest. Also He blesses them and they multiply greatly, and He does not let their cattle decrease. When they are diminished and bowed down through oppression, misery and sorrow, he pours contempt upon princes and makes them wander in a pathless waste. But He sets the needy securely on high away from affliction, and makes his families like a flock. The upright see it and are glad; but all unrighteousness shuts its mouth. Who is wise? Let

First, things change for those who are ungodly and promote wickedness. This passage says that rivers, a sign of life and fruitfulness, turn into a wilderness. Springs, another signal that life can exist, turn into dry ground. Fruitfulness turns into a salt waste. God's principal says that what productivity and life there is begins to dwindle away when He is not at the center of it.

The same passage, however, says that things are different for the godly. They find that even though they come into a wilderness, it becomes a pool of water. The dry land they have at the beginning becomes a spring. They are given the ability to establish cities, plant harvests and bring in food to feed their hungry bellies. It says specifically that the Lord blesses them and they grow in numbers. The Lord even watches over their cattle and does not let them decrease.

In this passage we see the godly being blessed, but those who are oppressing others wander in a pathless waste. The afflicted are sheltered and his family unit becomes like a flock, which the Lord tends Himself. Sometimes all this is taking place in the same country or city or even under one roof. One person might be sowing to self, greed and deceit and he or she is going to end up with a big pile of waste, going in circles, while another in the very same house is sowing to righteousness and ends up with fruitfulness, a river of delights and a spring of gladness welling up inside. How the Lord does this is so amazing to me.

Take, for instance, the story of Abraham and Lot in

Genesis. We read at the beginning that Lot chose the well-watered area that was like a garden, but the area he chose was sown to wickedness and Sodom and Gomorrah ended up a literal salt waste.

Abraham took the land that looked like a bad real estate deal, but ended up with a fruitful life continually watered by his relationship with the Lord. Were there deserts in the life of Abraham? Certainly there were. But the end product of daily walks with the Lord ended up planting a harvest of "I believe you, God" moments. Fulfilled promises were springing up like fountains even generations after his life was over.

This morning the Lord woke me up singing a song in my ear. That's the only way I can explain it. I was dead asleep and the moment I became conscious that I was awake, suddenly I had a phrase from the song "Open up The Heavens" running over and over through my mind. The bridge says, "Show us, show us Your glory" over and over again. And this, I feel, was the Lord beginning my day egging me on to beg Him to show me His glory. All during my quiet time in Isaiah chapter thirty-eight, I kept humming along with that part of the song, I felt its theme swelling within my heart, but I couldn't remember what the rest of the song was like or even which song the phrase came from when I first became aware of what I was humming. I looked through the most obvious place to solve the mystery… my itunes playlist entitled *Inner Court Worship*, which I frequently listen to while I am having my time with God. Nothing clicked and so I got lost reading about Hezekiah's sickness and the marvelous way that God commanded inanimate objects, like the shadow going back ten steps on the stairs. The thought kept hammering in on me that all these miraculous things happened just because Hezekiah took his boil to the Lord. God promised him several things--a heavenly prescription for healing, fifteen more years of fruitful living, deliverance from enemy number one and a promise of protection for his city. Does it get any better than that?

"Go and say to Hezekiah, Thus says the LORD, the God of David your father: I have heard your prayer, I have seen your tears; behold, I will add fifteen years to your life. I will deliver you and this city out of the hand of the king of Assyria, and defend this city. Isaiah 38:5-6 RSV

And so began a flaming hot time with God where He stirred up my heart to believe Him for big things for **my** day. He showed me how Hezekiah leveraged faithful obedience, not perfection, to ask humbly for more time to make a difference, and the Lord responded by indeed showing Hezekiah His glory in the midst of personal and national circumstances. The Lord and I had to talk about some bitter thoughts I was dealing with, His idea about my *"to do list"* for the day, and some situations where if healing didn't come, there would be death. I stumbled back into bed for my quiet had been VERY early in the morning and mumbled to Ike how good God had been to me in my quiet time. Later, when I got up for good, another part of the song was in my mind. This gave me enough words to Google it and I finally discovered what song it was from. I immediately began listening to it and worshipping the Lord through it.

You might think that my chapter got a bit off track here, but stay with me a moment. This is exactly what I am trying to illustrate. Just because you love God doesn't mean you're never going to suffer with a boil, or a bad

day, or end up on death's doorstep, or see an enemy invade your territory. But because Hezekiah was a
prayer warrior (go back to Isaiah 37 if you have doubts),
God took his personal Valley of Baca and turned it into
a place of springs.

How blessed is the man whose strength is in You,
in whose heart are the highways to Zion! Passing through
the valley of Baca they make it a spring; Psalm 84:5

Holman's Illustrated Bible says that Baca means weeping. The poet who penned the Psalm wanted us to know
that those who long to be in God's presence will have
places of weeping, like Hezekiah who turned his face to
the Lord and wept and prayed to the Lord – Isaiah 38:2,
but that daily intimacy with the Lord will turn that very
place into a place of springs.

In power the Lord helped me turn my bitter thoughts
over to be made into grace, He helped me to seek His
face in the midst of some difficult circumstances that
day and gave me hope for those who were at death's
door.

So stop for a moment and think about these words. Re-
flect on the fact that God is egging you on today, as
well. He wants you to ask Him to show you His glory. He's
singing it now in your ears:

Open up the Heavens
By Meredith Andrews
Album: **Worth it All**

We've waited for this day
We're gathered in your name

Calling out to you
Your glory like a fire
Awakening desire
Will burn our hearts with truth

You're the reason we're here
You're the reason we're singing

Open up the heavens
We want to see you
Open up the floodgates
A mighty river
Flowing from your heart
Filling every part of our praise

Your presence in this place
Your glory on our face
We're looking to the sky
Descending like a cloud
You're standing with us now
Lord, unveil our eyes

You're the reason we're here
You're the reason we're singing

Show us, show us your glory
Show us, show us your power
Show us, show us your glory, Lord

What will you bring to Him to transform today? He's egging you on to believe Him to do the great things, impossible things He does easily. Sing the song back to Him: ***Show us, show us your power.*** Begin to name the areas, the deserts you've seen lately that need water. The lives at death's door that could make use of fifteen more years of fruitfulness, and the boils on the body of Christ that are causing suffering. Picture the difference that Hezekiah's quiet time made and enjoy a flaming, red-hot prayer time with the One who has the power to turn the shadows back. You'll be singing His song for the rest of the day.

Chapter 7
Wonder of His Presence

Song of Solomon 2:3-5 As an apple tree among the trees of the wood, so is my beloved among young men. With great delight I sat in his shadow, and his fruit was sweet to my taste He brought me to the banqueting house, and his banner over me was love. Sustain me with raisins; refresh me with apples; for I am sick with love. RSV

Recently I started really eating a lot of apples. I was trying to eat healthier and so began my love affair with Fuji and McIntosh. Initially, when compared to chocolate chip cookies, pumpkin pie and tapioca pudding, these little *to go* packages of goodness didn't appeal much to me. They were too tart for my palette. But over time I have grown to love their juicy goodness. It just took time to develop my taste buds.

It's funny how a new perspective can change how you think about things. After fasting for a few days, the idea of biting into a juicy apple sounded so good. Sometimes now I just think to myself… "I could be fasting or I could be eating an apple." It helps draw me to the raw goodness that I would miss if I was longing for other things.

When I began working from home several months ago, another habit changed. I began to seek the Lord in a greater way. Several times a day, I would get alone with Him and read, pray and worship Him. I began to hunger for something deep and turned aside to spend time listening to a sermon, rather than be entertained. And here's what I discovered: my spiritual taste buds began to develop. I began to crave the juicy, wonder-working presence of God over relaxation, over the dry bread of what man's entertainment was offering me. As a result of my hunger and turning aside, the Lord began to do much more in my life. I felt a surge of spiritual power as the Lord began to speak to me about things from His Word; and as I chose to follow through on them, He blessed them.

The passage at the beginning of this chapter is a wonderful word picture of what began to happen. The Lord began giving me delightful morsels to feed my hunger for more of Him and to nourish me so I could pass on that refreshment to others. Solomon is using this word picture to ask God to sustain him and also to refresh him. Let me tell you, the Lord has all kinds of goodies and snacks to share, but first we have to be hungry enough to turn aside. We have to take great delight in His shade before his fruit can be sweet to our taste. Before He can hold our head with one hand and feed us with the other, we have to get used to taking daily picnics with Him.

So Moses said, "I must turn aside now and see this marvelous sight, why the bush is not burned up." When the Lord saw that he turned aside to look, God called to him from the midst of the bush and said, "Moses, Moses!" And he said, "Here I am." Exodus 3:3-4

It was after Moses made a decision to turn aside and see the sight that God spoke to him. God saw that he was seeking and God answered with a mighty buffet of His presence, and a message that would direct Moses' life for the next forty years. Do you hear Him whispering to your heart, "Turn aside and spend some time with me?" Your decision, your heart's appetite may direct what God has next in store for your life.

For bodily discipline is only of little profit, but godliness is profitable for all things, since it holds promise for the present life and also for the life to come. I Timothy 4:8

Oh my, the first morning I decided that I needed to do some sit ups each day, it was so comical. It wasn't a long session. It was actually quite pitiful. It was especially humorous since my husband was holding my feet and counting for me. In addition, my dog was giving me a lick for encouragement every time I made it up. But each morning that I have come to the place of grunting, it has been less painful. The exhilarating part came when I went to purchase some new pants and got to move down two sizes. Was it worth it to get down and go through the exercise each day? You bet it was.

Then came a day when I began to make new choices. A handful of cookies didn't look so good compared to moving down in a pant size. Although you can still catch me with a warm cookie in a weak moment, my snack of choice is definitely an apple.

I can enjoy this or that to read or watch, as well. But my snack of choice is to get alone with the Lord and sit in His shade tree and eat His one-of-a-kind delights, to hear His voice and enjoy His loving strength. If other things still sound better to you, turn aside, try out His raisin cakes and apples for a while. It won't be long until you get a hankering for His brand of refreshment that changes everything. There is nothing man can cook up that's even in the ballpark with his treats.

What do I mean by His snacks? It is God's Word speaking straight to me with power that sustains and refreshes my soul. It gives me energy during a difficult trial or time of waiting. His trail mix is ready to go and holds me on task while the trip gets wearisome. Try it. Just turn aside and begin reading His Word. I don't just mean by doing your regular Bible study. I mean just reading it for you and your circumstances at that moment. When the Lord highlights a verse, write it out on a 3x5 card and rubber band the collection as it begins to grow. Tired after a long day? Read through His Word for you and be suddenly refreshed. Then, this handy stack of verses to go will be available anytime you are floundering in your faith. When life's exertion taxes your momentum, pull out these little snack packs and be sustained and refreshed to continue the trail God has you on. You will also find direction for your life, comfort for your pain and treasures that thieves couldn't steal away if they tried. Just turn aside today and do some taste testing.

He who tends the fig tree will eat its fruit, and he who cares for his master will be honored. Proverbs 27:18

When we turn aside to spend time with our Lord, He always blesses us. But there is even a better motivation, when we turn aside simply to be with Him, to bless His name, to adore His great power, His gift to us becomes **His very presence**. This is true worship. It's sweet perfume to His nostrils. He is a great King and deserves our highest praise and adoration. So many are running to and fro and are becoming spiritually emaciated. As they run, looking for strength, they become tired, parched and weary. When we simply desire to be with Him, He shares His strength and His presence with us. Nothing is more satisfying.

But know that the Lord has set apart the godly man for Himself; the Lord hears when I call to Him. Psalm 4:3

But his delight is in the law of the Lord, and in His law he meditates day and night. He will be like a tree firmly planted by streams of water, which yields its fruit in its season and its leaf does not wither; and in whatever he does, he prospers. Psalm 1:2-3

For He has satisfied the thirsty soul, and the hungry soul He has filled with what is good. Psalm 107:9

But his delight is in the law of the Lord, and in His law he meditates day and night. He will be like a tree firmly planted by streams of water, which yields its fruit in its season and its leaf does not wither; and in whatever he does, he prospers. Psalm 1:2-3

The benefit to enjoying His presence is that when we spend regular quality time with our Lord, it isn't long before He wants to show us something He's been working on. We might get a little look at some blueprints He's been drawing up, or something He's been fiddling on in His workshop. We will also find that just a word from Him is exactly what we've needed for a few projects of our own. You can't enjoy God's presence without this exchange happening.

My daughter Mary and I pray each week at our church on Saturday mornings. We walk the perimeter of the property, and, of course, we verbalize all the areas where we need our Savior's help. I can't think of a day when we haven't left that spot and gone on to the other tasks of the day without new zeal and ideas. It just happens. In His presence we find strength, direction and peace. Haven't I made your mouth water just talking about it?

"Draw me after you and let us run together! The king has brought me into his chambers." Song of Solomon 1:4

Who have I in heaven but you? And besides You, I desire nothing on earth. Psalm 73:25

But as for me, the nearness of God is my good; I have made the Lord God my refuge, That I may tell of all Your works. Psalm 73:28

For the devious are an abomination to the Lord; but He is intimate with the upright. Proverbs 3:32

You will make known to me the path of life; In Your presence is fullness of joy; In Your right hand there are pleasures forever. Psalm 16:11

But only a few things are necessary, really only one, for Mary has chosen the good part, which shall not be taken away from her. Luke 10:42

Chapter 8
Wonder of His Purposes

I have decided one thing for certain: I am never going to be able to figure God out. For the last eight years of my life, I have lived life at break neck speed. My job of teaching at a Christian school felt like Nehemiah's task of rebuilding the walls, and there didn't ever seem time enough to rest. However, after resigning that position by His release, for the last several months, the Lord has had me in a holding pattern: be still, listen, read, pray, wait, and repeat. There has been no way out of this call on my life for this season. Believe me, some days I've tried.

While *I've been* in this holding tank, He has been asking me to trust Him for what I can't see and don't understand. He made it clear through some scriptures that He gave me to hold onto during this time, that I'm not designed to be able to figure out what He's doing.

If no one knows what will happen, who can tell him when it will happen? Ecclesiastes 8:7

Just as you do not know the path of the wind and how bones are formed in the womb of the pregnant woman, so you do not know the activity of God who makes all things. Ecclesiastes 11:5

Why should the nations say, "Where, now, is their God?" But our God is in the heavens; He does whatever He pleases.
Psalm 115:2-3

Man's steps are ordained by the Lord, How then can man understand his way? Proverbs 20:24

Consider the work of God, for who is able to straighten what He has bent? Ecclesiastes 7:13

There is one way that God and I are alike. We both like to do what we want. The way we are different is that I don't always get to do what I want. Today I was wishing I could buy a new computer because mine was running slower than a snail skating on a pile of molasses, but my bank account replied that there were some limits to my wishing. The Lord does not suffer from the limits of resources. There has never been a desire in Him that was held back by supply.

"For every beast of the forest is Mine, The cattle on a thousand hills. I know every bird of the mountains, and everything that moves in the field is Mine. If I were hungry I would not tell you, for the world is Mine, and all it contains." Psalm 50:10-12

Some days I wish to be eloquent and brilliant. It's easy to see I don't always get what I want in that department either. My thoughts are greatly limited by my memory, my capacity to reason and the information I have available. But God has never felt those limitations. His has an unlimited amount of knowledge on any subject available at any moment.

How great are Your works, O Lord! Your thoughts are very deep. Psalm 92:5

"For as the heavens are higher than the earth, so are My ways higher than your ways and My thoughts than your thoughts. Isaiah 55:9

Even the span of time does not limit Him. The One who stopped the sun for Joshua and turned back the shadow on the stairs for Hezekiah understands that all things are His servants. His creation and everything in it stand ready to serve Him. From a fish, a worm and a plant in the book of Jonah, to a raven, a jar of oil and some flour in the book of Kings, everything serves Him at His mere whim. He says in Isaiah 5:26 and 7:18 that He whistles, and a nation moves.

He will also lift up a standard to the distant nation, and will whistle for it from the ends of the earth; and behold, it will come with speed swiftly. Isaiah 5:26

In that day the Lord will whistle for the fly that is in the remotest part of the rivers of Egypt and for the bee that is in the land of Assyria. Isaiah 7:18

On occasion I want to be strong enough to move something without waiting around for help. But there have been some times where I have realized I simply don't have the power to complete my will. God on the other hand can wish it and do it simultaneously. He has the power to bend something or change something so that no one can ever straighten it again. He can move a mountain or a debt that seems as high as a mountain. He can shrivel up a fig tree and cause it to never bear again. By His mere look all of creation trembles. By His Word the pattern of the universe was set in motion.

He looks at the earth, and it trembles; He touches the mountains, and they smoke. Psalm 104:32

Thou hast a strong arm; Thy hand is mighty Your right hand is exalted. Psalm 89:13

For He spoke, and it was done; He commanded, and it stood fast. Psalm 33:9

"But He is unique and who can turn Him? And what His soul desires, that He does." For He performs what is appointed for me, and many such decrees are with Him. Job 23:13-14

I am limited and will never understand all that God knows and is doing. However, there is one thought that I can center in on during this time of waiting: God is orchestrating this time for my good. Of this I can be totally sure.

As I look back on some of the hardest times in my life, I realize that in the midst of dark days, God was teaching me, loving me and protecting me. The things He saw might have been more dangerous than I understood. His whisking me away from danger could be viewed in my mind as keeping me from stuff I love and to Him, the same event might have been protection from destruction.

Perspective is so helpful in making an attitude adjustment. If I spend this time convinced of God's love and care, then all the mental ups and down on this stationary journey will feel comforting rather than confining.

I have thought during this time that perhaps the Lord has given me this time to enjoy more time with my husband and with Him. We never know when a person might be whisked out of our lives, and we must enjoy the time we have with them. Perhaps the Lord is accomplishing something (like the writing of this book) that might never get done if I were at my normal pace of activity. Perhaps the Lord wants me to hear His whisper and I need to get quiet enough to hear it. Who knows? Like I said, I will never figure Him out. But again, why do I need to try to figure Him out? He's got this handled. I can just sit back and rest in His strength, His wisdom and His love.

But as for me, I trust in You, O Lord, I say, "You are my God." My times are in Your hand; deliver me from the hand of my enemies and from those who persecute me. Psalm 31:14-15

So he shepherded them according to the integrity of his heart, and guided them with his skillful hands. Psalm 78:72

Chapter 9
Wonder of His Priorities

I felt called to serve the Lord early in life. There have been many times when I have been actually employed as a church or Christian school employee. But there have also been times when I was in between ministry assignments. During those times, I viewed myself as being an employee of the Lord. I didn't necessarily receive a regular paycheck, but I did learn that the Lord can take care of my needs one way or another. He is not limited to a W-2 or a 1099.

During the latest transition time, I became more and more interested in things that I thought the Lord felt were valuable uses of my time. I found through reading scripture that the Lord was keenly interested in my care and concern for those who could not repay me. An earthly boss might have been impressed with working late; however, my Heavenly Boss was more interested in how I checked in on the helpless, the weary and the overwhelmed.

It felt to me that when I encouraged the downhearted, I was getting a "thumbs up" from Him. Taking time to write a note or make a phone call to pray with someone going through a difficult trial began to give me more of a rush than getting a gold star on a review.

It is interesting when you begin to think of yourself in this way. There may be down time during the day and then you may be called to pray or read or write in the middle of the night. It's interesting. There may be little "work" for a couple of days and then a barrage of ministry activity. I smile, knowing that with this job, I am on call and can have some interesting work hours...like an obstetrician or a paramedic.

As I read the Word, I began to see more than ever a trend in God's priorities for His children. He is very much interested when we care for the lonely, the depressed, and the downtrodden. In an age when everyone **can** be connected, few are. This is a tool of the enemy who knows that disconnected servants are easy prey. I began to see that in a way as an encourager I had the ability to even the odds.

Deliver those who are being taken away to death, and those who are staggering to slaughter, oh hold them back. If you say, "See, we did not know this," Does He not consider it who weighs the hearts? And does He not know it who keeps your soul? And will He not render to man according to his work? Proverbs 24:11-12

Then I looked again at all the acts of oppression which were being done under the sun. And behold I saw the tears of the oppressed and that they had no one to comfort them; and on the side of their oppressors was power, but they had no one to comfort them. Ecclesiastes 4:1

These are some of the verses that were impressed on my heart and these words were seared into me by the Lord.

When I really look and really see, I can see lots that are under a heavy load. When I take the time to really focus in on the needs of others, I see that they don't have anyone to comfort them. And yes, their oppressor has power, but they need comfort.

Now I freely admit that I will not humanly be able to comfort all those that need encouragement. But what I can do is to take the time to look and really see. And when the Lord, the God of all comfort, shows me someone who needs some help, and He gives me something to share with them, I can do it. After all, that's why I'm on His payroll.

A good example was when I saw a friend on Facebook who I know has a marvelous gift of preaching. Right now he has a wagonload of kids, a full time job and very little outlet for his gift. I reminded him that I am still profoundly touched by the times I have heard him speak. It helped.

I love the verses that follow. In leading a Bible study recently, I saw an overwhelming need for our Savior's strength. As we shared our personal struggles, it was evident that we had enough need in that little room for a hundred people. We needed strength. As I meditated on this set of verses, the Lord reminded me that He saw our need, as well, and that He was going to answer the need Himself. Love it!

"The afflicted and needy are seeking water, but there is none, and their tongue is parched with thirst;
I, the LORD, will answer them Myself, As the God of Israel I will not forsake them. "I will open rivers on the bare heights and springs in the midst of the valleys;

I will make the wilderness a pool of water and the dry land fountains of water. "I will put the cedar in the wilderness,

The acacia and the myrtle and the olive tree; I will place the juniper in the desert Together with the box tree and the cypress, That they may see and recognize, And consider and gain insight as well, that the hand of the LORD has done this,

And the Holy One of Israel has created it. Isaiah 41:17-20

This resulted in a new sense of purpose for me. I began to see that many people could do a lot of things. But that I had been especially created to encourage others. It came so naturally to me. Yes, the Lord was meeting the need of His people, but he was using me as the clay pipe to get them their refreshment. I began to go deeper into praying for others, reminding the Lord that He had promised to "answer them Himself." And I got the joy of having His spirit pass through me and my little "part" of the process.

"I am the LORD, I have called You in righteousness, I will also hold You by the hand and watch over You, and I will appoint You as a covenant to the people, as a light to the nations, to open blind eyes, to bring out prisoners from the dungeon and those who dwell in darkness from the prison. I am the LORD, that is My name; I will not give My glory to another, nor My praise to graven images. Behold, the former things have come to pass, now I declare new things; before they spring forth I proclaim them to you." Isaiah 42:6-9

Hear, you deaf! And look, you blind, that you may see.

Who is blind but My servant, or so deaf as My messenger whom I send? Who is so blind as he that is at peace with Me, or so blind as the servant of the LORD? You have seen many things, but you do not observe them; your ears are open, but none hears. The LORD was pleased for His righteousness' sake to make the law great and glorious. But this is a people plundered and despoiled; all of them are trapped in caves, or are hidden away in prisons; they have become a prey with none to deliver them, and a spoil, with none to say, "Give them back!" Isaiah 42:18-22

Saying to those who are bound, 'Go forth,' To those who are in darkness, 'Show yourselves.' Along the roads they will feed, and their pasture will be on all bare heights. Isaiah 49:10

"They will not hunger or thirst, nor will the scorching heat or sun strike them down; for He who has compassion on them will lead them and will guide them to springs of water. Isaiah 49:9

The Lord GOD has given Me the tongue of disciples, that I may know how to sustain the weary one with a word. He awakens me morning by morning, He awakens my ear to listen as a disciple. Isaiah 50:4

Now I know that this journey is not unique to me. I see other encouragers around. I see their posts on Facebook and Twitter. I see them linger on Sundays to pray with others. I see their cards hung on refrigerators and mantles. And I want to challenge those of you who have not seen this calling yet. Spiritual revival can come at the ministry of preachers and evangelists, but it can also come from loving hearts who reach out. How about you? Would you like to be one of God's employees? There are wonderful job benefits: one on one time in the head office with the boss and his personal mentorship program, a salary guaranteed to meet your needs, a creative and challenging work environment, long term security and more.

Is there any downside of working for the Lord? There is only one I can think of: You don't get the benefit ever of saying, "No" to any work related assignment. Because the Lord knows your abilities, HIS abilities, and can manipulate time, space and nature to help you meet His deadlines, there are no excuses for not following through on His impulses. When you consider that He will prompt you, strengthen you, encourage you and help you, who wouldn't want to be on His payroll?

Not sure if you can do this job? Why not try it out today. Look around...try to see those around you that could use some living water, some refreshment, a thought from God's Word to help them through their day. Send them an email, a tweet, or give them a call. I'm sure you'll get hooked.

Bring out the people who are blind, even though they have eyes, and the deaf, even though they have ears. Isaiah 43:8

"Is this not the fast which I choose, to loosen the bonds of wickedness, to undo the bands of the yoke, and to let the oppressed go free and break every yoke? "Is it not to divide your bread with the hungry and bring the homeless poor into the house; when you see the naked, to cover him; and not to hide yourself from your own flesh? "Then your light will break out like the dawn, and

your recovery will speedily spring forth; and your righteousness will go before you; the glory of the LORD will be your rear guard. "Then you will call, and the LORD will answer; you will cry, and He will say, 'Here I am.' If you remove the yoke from your midst, The pointing of the finger and speaking wickedness, and if you give yourself to the hungry and satisfy the desire of the afflicted, then your light will rise in darkness and your gloom will become like midday. "And the LORD will continually guide you, satisfy your desire in scorched places, and give strength to your bones; and you will be like a watered garden, and like a spring of water whose waters do not fail. Isaiah 58:6-11

"Arise, shine; for your light has come, and the glory of the LORD has risen upon you. For behold, darkness will cover the earth and deep darkness the peoples; but the LORD will rise upon you and His glory will appear upon you. Nations will come to your light, and kings to the brightness of your rising." Isaiah 60:1-3

Chapter 10
Wonder of His Prophetic Word

At age seventeen, Joseph is the recipient of a wonderful prophetic promise of an event that will take place later in his life. He has a dream, one of many, in which the Lord reveals something up ahead. I must surmise that Joseph believed God's Word to him, because later, he shares it with his family. He declares something God has revealed that could bring him ridicule. I believe their taunting comes not because he **had** a dream, but because his family sees that he really **believes** it. In this dream, Joseph sees his family bowing down to him.

At this time, nothing could be further from the reality of his circumstance. His brothers are days away from selling him into slavery and are seriously entertaining the thought of murdering him. Given the state of Joseph's current conditions, I think it is easy to see this dream did not come from his own mind and heart.

This kind of dream rises above what we could ever simply "hope" for. It is greater than our human thoughts. I don't believe that even Joseph would have aspired to surpass ten brothers, older than him, in authority and honor.

Joseph has to wade through a whole lot of junk before light arises to the promise. How many times did Joseph turn to the Lord and say, "But You said, Lord?" How many times did the Lord press the thought of the dream again into Joseph's thinking, when there was no human chance of its fulfillment, so He could see if Joseph would believe still?

Yet true to his Word, the day comes when as Pharaoh's second hand man, all his brothers come to buy food and bow down to him. Now, I believe Joseph was moved, as scripture says, to see Benjamin again. But I can't but help think that some of his tears were because a partial fulfillment of God's prophetic dream was taking place when eleven strong willed brothers bowed the knee to honor him.

A study of Abraham reveals that several times after his promise of a son, the Lord brought up the promise to see if Abraham would believe Him. Even Sarah got a chance to "believe." We are told in the New Testament that Abraham, when he considered his own body, as good as dead, believed God's promise. Sarah too had times of faith because she is mentioned in the Hall of Faith as having believed.

Saying, I will surely bless you, and I will surely multiply you, and thus, having patiently waited he obtained the promise. Hebrews 6:14-15

I have had similar experiences. Funny, I did not dream that the sun moon and stars would bow down to me. But on one occasion, while worshipping, I saw an unsaved friend beaming with a joy that I felt could only come from an encounter with the Lord. It was at that moment that I believed the Lord was showing me that my friend, Joe Branchaud, the father of a close friend, would become a Christian. This presented somewhat of a problem because at the time, Joe was a professed atheist. I shared the incident with my friend, her brother, and Joe's wife. They had been praying for years for Joe. I realized that sharing this "vision" could bring ridicule, but I felt that the Lord needed to see my faith in the midst of the situation.

It was several years before we saw a little movement in Joe's life. He now told his family that he was an agnostic. A few years after that, he began attending church, mainly to see the grandchildren performing in programs and such. But later Joe did regularly come to worship services, though in private, he still argued issues with his family members and had made no profession of faith.

Unbelief continually asks, "How can this be possible?" It is always full of "how's," yet faith needs only one great answer to every ten thousand of "how's." That answer is---GOD! C.H.M. p. 249, **Streams in the Desert**, *Updated edition. Edited James Reimann.*

During the time we "waited" on the Lord, there were times in my prayer closet, that the Lord pressed in on me to believe His Word to me. There were times of deep intercession where I pleaded for Joe's salvation. One Sunday morning, during worship, I felt such a grieving spirit rest on me that I wept tears over his stubbornness to accept Christ. The Holy Spirit who resided in me was grieving through me for Joe's resistance.

Eight years later Joe called. He had finally accepted the Lord. What a wonderful moment that was! His family told me with tears of the first time Joe had ever prayed out loud with them.

Why am I choosing to include this subject in a book on prayer? It is because I believe that as you grow in your prayer time, you may have similar experiences. I have had several in my life. These were impossible situations where God revealed His will to me early on in the process so that I would partner with Him. But it took time between the proclamation and the fulfillment of His Word to see their fulfillment.

I believe at these times, that you will need to nurture your faith on a regular basis. The waiting time can end up being so much longer than we envision. You may be invited by the Lord to labor in bringing about the fulfillment of that promise. But, oh the joy of seeing the miraculous happen and to know that God has helped you believe Him to do it!

When Joe began walking with God, I began to think: "Who else does the Lord want to save that I just haven't had the faith to ask Him to save?" Today, make that your prayer.

Prayer is insisting upon Jesus' victory and the retreat of the enemy on each particular spot and heart problem concerned. S.D. Gordon

All the powers of evil seek to hinder our prayer life because prayer, by nature, involves conflict with opposing forces. May God give us grace to strive in prayer until we prevail. Andrew Murray

Chapter 11
Wonder of His Faith

I thought this book was all sealed up and finished until this morning. A couple of days ago, I had opened my Sunday School lesson to work and the Lord let loose a barn burner on me, as my husband would call it. That's a message that burns itself into your heart and you know it's going to get preached one way or another. That's why the Lord seared it into you. Then this morning came His voice, "Put it in the book." "OK, Lord."

"All the commandments that I am commanding you today you shall be careful to do, that you may live and multiply, and go in and possess the land which the LORD swore to give to your forefathers. You shall remember all the way which the LORD your God has led you in the wilderness these forty years, that He might humble you, testing you, to know what was in your heart, whether you would keep His commandments or not. He humbled you and let you be hungry, and fed you with manna which you did not know, nor did your fathers know, that He might make you understand that man does not live by bread alone, but man lives by everything that proceeds out of the mouth of the LORD. Your clothing did not wear out on you, nor did your foot swell these forty years. Thus you are to know in your heart that the LORD your God was disciplining you just as a man disciplines

his son. Therefore, you shall keep the commandments of the LORD your God, to walk in His ways and to fear Him. For the LORD your God is bringing you into a good land, a land of brooks of water, of fountains and springs, flowing forth in valleys and hills; a land of wheat and barley, of vines and fig trees and pomegranates, a land of olive oil and honey; a land where you will eat food without scarcity, in which you will not lack anything; a land whose stones are iron, and out of whose hills you can dig copper. When you have eaten and are satisfied, you shall bless the LORD your God for the good land which He has given you. "Beware that you do not forget the LORD your God by not keeping His commandments and His ordinances and His statutes which I am commanding you today; otherwise, when you have eaten and are satisfied, and have built good houses and lived in them, and when your herds and your flocks multiply, and your silver and gold multiply, and all that you have multiplies, then your heart will become proud and you will forget the LORD your God who brought you out from the land of Egypt, out of the house of slavery. He led you through the great and terrible wilderness, with its fiery serpents and scorpions and thirsty ground where there was no water; He brought water for you out of the rock of flint. In the wilderness He fed you manna which your fathers did not know, that He might humble you and that He might test you, to do good for you in the end. Otherwise, you may say in your heart, 'My power and the strength of my hand made me this wealth.' But you shall remember the LORD your God, for it is He who is giving you power to make wealth, that He may confirm His covenant which He swore to your fathers, as it is this day. It shall come about if you ever forget the LORD your God and go after other gods and serve them and worship them, I testify against you today that you will surely perish. Deut. 8:1-19

Today will affect your tomorrow. God wants you to live, and multiply and possess the land that He has set aside and declared to be yours. That "land" is not a piece of property, but a way of life where His name is over you, your community and your nation. But that will be impossible without passing through the wilderness, which is a season of testing.

The Lord wants you to see, like a good coach, where He is taking you. He tells us in verse seven that it is a good land, a land with brooks, fountains and springs that flow forth to saturate the valleys and the hills. A land where He says, "You will never know lack." In this Promised Land life will be better. But in order to get there, you're going to have to pass through a place you'd rather not visit: the wilderness. There is no way to that place without traveling through this kind of a place.

The wilderness season has a purpose. God says there are several things that must happen for you to live in that promised place in the future:

You must experience God's authority over all things.
   Clothing that doesn't wear out.
   Your foot not swelling.
   A cloud that moves by day/a pillar of fire by night.
   A rock that gushes water.
   Manna provision that comes at appointed times.

What do all these things have in common? They are things that are completely opposite to the way things normally happen. Why? Because the Lord wants you to see that He controls all things. If He doesn't control it all, He's not God.

The Lord tells us in verse sixteen that He wants to do good for us in the end. But in order to get there, we have to pass through the place where there is nothing BUT God.

There have been a couple of times in my life that I would consider a wilderness. As I look back, these changes in my "normal" were so that I would learn to hunger for His presence and live by His Word. They were also so I would learn that God could do the impossible when it suits His purpose.

We must experience a humbling season so we will learn to live by His Word. The Lord uses the word "discipline" in this passage. His discipline comes not because you have been bad, but so that you can experience the good. You are the child raised to know how to live better.

You've seen them...children who eat junk food all day and watch horrible TV. But you are God's child and you are being trained for a better, healthier way. But you don't get that way naturally. You must be trained. That is the sense here. God, Your Father, wants to train you to have a taste for better spiritual food, a better way of life, a higher purpose. He wants you to learn to live by His commands instead of your own desires. He wants you to learn to move at His impulse.

You must experience lack to find gain. Food (or a paycheck) might have to go away so that you will see God as the source of your life. You must taste manna so you understand that it is real life. God's Word declares truth and when that looks completely opposite to your circumstance and you choose to live daily in its truth, you find real life.

The wilderness is no fun, but what we learn there solidifies in our hearts that God is really God and must be feared, honored and obeyed. And that is the good land. When we figure it out, when we understand in our belly that without Him we couldn't eat or live or accomplish one picking thing…we enter the good land where we learn to really live and multiply and have no lack.

He says in verse seventeen that otherwise, without the wilderness, we might think WE got there by our own power and strength. That it was OUR hand that got us there. That's why the path through the *Wilderness of Only What God Provides* is essential, and that's why remembering what we learned there is so important.

So today, God says, "I want to take you there. The Promised Land. I know it is possible. You're not there yet. All the good you think you already know is really nothing in comparison to what's up ahead. But to get from here to there, I'm going to have to take you to some scary places where you don't have any other options except to rely on me so you can find out that I'm the only option you need. I want to teach you that when I say something, you can bet your life on it. Even if NOTHING in the physical says that's even possible. Remember, I can take a rock and make water gush.

Conclusion

Get ready to see things unimaginable!

When you get your heart settled down enough to hear God's voice, and by the way, that can happen in one second in case you were thinking you didn't have time. When your spiritual appetite gets hungry enough that no other diet can satisfy you like His presence, and by the way, that can happen the instant you turn away from the world's junk food and sit down at His table ready to eat. Some will be just little tufting clouds of promise off in the distance after much intercession. Some will be answered so quickly that you will barely get the words out of your mouth before you see His response. But you, like me, will be ruined for every other kind of activity. You will want to linger in His workshop, fingering His plans sketched out on the pages of His Word, and watching as He constructs things that take your breath away.

It is there that you will watch with wonder as the Creator of the Universe intervenes in the lives of His children with the tools of love, mercy and faithfulness. And it's a sure thing that at some point you will think, "I wonder if He wants to do this…" To which He may respond, "I've just been waiting for you to ask." And another jaw- dropping moment of wonder will begin.